ADD to Excellent Without Drugs

Meredith Day

ADD to Excellent Without Drugs

Published by:
BLUE BIRD PUBLISHING
2266 S. Dobson, Suite #275
Mesa AZ 85202
(602) 831-6063 FAX (602) 831-1829
Email: bluebird@bluebird1.com
Web site: http://www.bluebird1.com

Printed in the United States of America
ISBN 0-933025-62-9 $12.95
Cover Design by James Esker

Disclaimer

The information contained in this book is not intended to be a substitute for medical advice. Before making any drastic changes in diet or lifestyle, consult a physician. The Detox Diet in this book is recommended only for adults, and only after consulting a physician.

About the Author

Meredith Day, a third generation movie industry brat, has spent 30 years researching parenting and hyperactive children. A hyperactive child herself, she developed *ADD to Excellent Without Drugs* initially for her own salvation. Through her work as an Entertainment Industry Talent Manager, she interacts daily with children and adults from all backgrounds. Because entertainment careers are so chaotic and demanding, Ms. Day uses her *ADD to Excellent Without Drugs* techniques to guide adult actors and the parents of young actors in stress survival.

Meredith Day lives in Encinitas, California, with her son. She not only manages entertainment talent, but also pens motion picture and television music and screenplays.

Table of Contents

Introduction

ADD To Excellent is an operations guide for the parent who wants to explore alternatives to chemical therapy for their hyperactive or attention deficit child. The Ground Zero Program has been used successfully not only with school age children, but ADD Adults as well.

In the 90s there has been a severe rise in the diagnosis of ADD or ADHD among school age children and the prescription of Ritalin, and other stimulants as corrective therapy for misbehavior in the school environment.

Many times a core trigger of this disorder has been completely ignored or overlooked. Whether ADD/ADHD is an actual isolateable gene, or a chemical imbalance in the front of the brain, before arbitrarily throwing a child on drug therapy the child should be taken to nutritional "Ground Zero" to assess if they are able to function normally without chemical intervention.

ADD To Excellent will also help a parent determine if a child does have the genetic or chemical predisposition toward ADD or ADHD, or if the child is overly bright and merely bored in the traditional school environment.

ADD To Excellent is dedicated to our future, and the children that we will depend on to lead us into the next century.

- 1 -

What is ADD (ADHD/ADLD)?

ADD= Attention Deficit Disorder

For years this was the catch all for anyone exhibiting dysfunctional hyperactive behavior.

ADHD= Attention Deficit Hyperactive Disorder

This is the term most commonly used today to define a dysfunctional hyperactive child or adult. The hyperactive symptoms show up 3 to 1 males over females.

ADLD= Attention Deficit Lethargic Disorder

Predominately affecting females, the primary ADD triggers such as sugar and caffeine abuse show up, not as hyperactivity, but as lethargy, extreme exhaustion. The ADLD will commonly not be disruptive, but will be a "daydreamer", be off task and often sleep through classes or work. The ADLD sleeps long hours and is hard to wake up. After meals they will feel exhausted and find it very difficult to finish even small tasks. In the adult ADLD exhaustion usually sets in shortly after meals, and continues throughout the day. This makes working an almost insurmountable task when the sufferer would rather just go to bed.

WHAT IS ADD (ADHD/ADLD)

Years ago hyperactive children were called rambunctious or rabble rousers. In every school classroom there was a troublemaker, a class clown, and a dreamer. These unruly or uncooperative children often went on to make great contributions to our society. Good examples are John Paul Getty and Albert Einstein. In the old days the school's solution to keeping these children in line was corporal punishment and very strict discipline.

Punishment for classroom misbehavior included slapping the child on the knuckles with a ruler, or a paddling by the educator to keep the hyperactive child in control. Many times the solution was to keep the child after school writing hundreds of apologetic sentences on the black board, or put him on display on a tall stool in a dunce cap at the front of the class.

This old fashioned standard of treatment often caused the highly creative or highly intelligent student to drop out of school. They would make their way in the world naturally floating up to the top level, as in the case of John Paul Getty.

Though this old fashioned type of school discipline is greatly frowned on, and in many states currently against the law, it did keep the offending children in order in the classroom. When faced with a greater evil, the smart child ceased the disruptive behavior, or got out. Classrooms were generally quiet and well ordered. There was no back talk or disruptive behavior allowed.

These days educators have no effective recourse against the disruptive child. Classrooms are overcrowded. The percentage of learning compared to the onerous job of keeping order with little or no effective tools of discipline is highly out of balance. It is not uncommon to see a single teacher supervising a classroom of as many as 32 young poorly disciplined children.

At the same time, technology is having a marked effect on our children. With the advent of fast paced video games, television and MTV, the brain synapses that enable a child to think at light speed and perfect the lightning fast motor reflexes to excel at video games are sometimes a contributing factor to a child's classroom car wreck.

Brain synapses are the connections that develop when the individual is forced to function in a new manner. An example is children that are raised in multilingual families. Their brains develop connections to recognize both language sound patterns. This is why a bilingual child can go forward and much more easily adopt third and fourth languages. His brain has developed the synapse connections to hear and understand a variety of different sound patterns.

By the same token, a child that is able to act and think at high speed can grasp concepts much quicker, and also becomes bored quickly without the high level of stimulation their brain has evolved to accept.

While our children are developing highly evolved motor and thinking skills, they are also being assailed by drug overdoses via their daily diet. These are drugs such as sugar, caffeine and preservatives. Each child's metabolism reacts differently. Some children can ingest these drugs with no visible results. Others have such a high intolerance to the drugs that their reaction is way off the chart with the most minimal exposure.

There is much debate about what causes ADD or as it is now fashionable to call it, ADHD. One school of thought is that there is a chemical imbalance in the front of the brain which causes inappropriate activity, lack of focus and brain dysfunction. Another quadrant believes that there is an actual isolatable gene that is the root cause of the syndrome.

The symptoms of the syndrome vary greatly. The most noticeable are those individuals who are hyperactive, disruptive, and have a violent temper—the high ups and severe downs. Those not able to remember or follow the most elementary instruction. Handwriting disability is thought to be a major defining symptom of ADD.

There are other more subtle sufferers. Those that are

unable to stay awake in class. They suffer from continual daydreams. They cannot focus on tasks for long periods of time. They forget what they are doing, they find it impossible to keep their brain in the classroom. They feel constantly exhausted. They can't wait to go to bed, and are almost impossible to wake up in the morning. These victims do not disrupt others, but they derail their own lives, having great difficulty attaining success. They feel like they're running to catch up all their lives.

Attention Deficit Hyperactive Disorder (ADHD) is much more common in males where Attention Deficit Lethargic Disorder (ADLD) affects more females. This fact is not reported as often due to the fact ADLDs are much less likely to disrupt those around them, and therefore are many times overlooked, undiagnosed.

Sufferers of ADD often feel substandard or worthless, they can't understand why they are incapable of doing simple tasks that come easily to their friends or business associates. They have no self esteem. Before and after they are diagnosed, they suffer derision, taunts and anger from parents and peers. A normally functioning parent cannot understand why Johnny takes hours to do homework that other siblings can accomplish in a half hour. They can't understand why he constantly wanders away from his task. They can't understand why they can't get him to buckle down. When held up against non-ADD siblings, the child suffers derision that that is the foundation of his opinion of himself and impacts him for the rest of his life. "Why can't you be good like your sister/brother?"

Whether the ADD Syndrome is caused by a chemical imbalance in the brain or a genetic disorder, the truth is that these individuals react severely to the ingestion of certain chemicals. The most common is sugar, followed by caffeine and preservatives. Humorously, some doctors actually instruct parents of such children on masking drugs such as Ritalin to administer caffeine as a remedy at times of "blow out".

If the child's brain reacts adversely to certain substances, those substances must be deleted from the child's diet. In case studies we have found an overwhelming number of the children diagnosed with ADD can be virtually cured by mere diet adjustment. Sadly this is the last thing to be addressed by many psychologists and physicians. Unfortunately these highly qualified professionals have learned by experience that it takes a caring and dedicated parent to go through the difficulty of deprogramming and detoxing their child. Many times the foods that are adversely affecting the child are the parents' favorite treats, and they are unwilling to delete them from the household. It is much easier to administer drugs and therapy to their child than to disrupt their own dietary lifestyle.

Deprogramming doesn't mean the child is cured. The child will be sensitive to certain chemical substances for the rest of his life. It does mean, however, that the child can, with the proper diet, live a normal and productive life.

This book is written for the passionate caring parent. The parent who wants to truly qualify whether their child needs chemical intervention with behavior masking drugs and therapy. Does the child need merely a change in diet to function as a pleasant and productive human being? Does he need more stimulation at school? Does he need a vision or hearing problem diagnosed and treated?

ADD To Excellent is for the parent who is willing to move heaven and earth to give their child the gift of a healthy, happy and productive future.

THE CLASSIC SYMPTOMS OF ADD

The following are symptoms that are thought to indicate ADD (ADHD or ADLD). Deleting the triggers will, in most cases, cause the symptoms to disappear.

1. A diet full of sugar and caffeine.

A. Hyperactivity
B. Excessive crankiness
C. Exhaustion
D. Excessive talking
E. Inability to retain verbal instructions
F. Physical violence
G. Lack of memory retention
H. Recurring vaginitis
I. Breast lumps (caffeine)
J. Cannot stay on task
K. Recurring headaches
L. Handwriting impairment
M.Reading disability
N. Mathematics disability, cannot retain facts
O. Memorization impairment
P. Daydreaming
Q. Reacts violently to peer teasing
R. Frequent crying

2. Boredom due to high IQ

A. Hyperactivity
B. Disruptive schoolroom behavior
C. Lack of schoolroom focus
D. Excessive talking
E. Excessive frustration (short fuse)
F. Cannot stay on task
G. Interrupts in the middle of a sentence
H. Daydreaming

I. Excessive anger
J. Reacts violently to peer teasing

3. Learning-related visual impairment

A. Hyperactivity
B. Holds head at odd angle when reading
C. Recurring headaches
D. Reading disability
E. Handwriting disability
F. Squinting
G. Excessive frustration
H. Reacts violently to peer teasing
I. Anger
J. Cannot stay on task

4. Hearing impairment.

A. Hyperactivity
B. "Does not listen"
C. Incessantly asks, "What?"
D. Turns head to one side to listen
E. Does not obey verbal commands
F. Scores poorly in classroom discussion
G. Excessive frustration
H. Anger
I. Speaks unclearly
J. Reacts violently to peer teasing
K. Cannot stay on task

5. Hand to brain motor impairment.

A. Hyperactivity
B. Handwriting impairment
C. Cannot complete written assignments
D. Leaves words or letters out of written assignments.
E. Scores poorly on oral dictation
F. Excessive frustration
G. Anger

H. Reacts violently to peer teasing
I. Cannot stay on task

6. Hypoglycemia and diabetes

A. Hyperactivity
B. Excessive crankiness
C. Exhaustion
D. Excessive talking
E. Inability to retain verbal instructions
F. Physical violence
G. Lack of memory retention
H. Cannot stay on task
I. Recurring headaches
J. Handwriting impairment
K. Reading disability
L. Mathematics disability, cannot retain facts
M. Memorization impairment
N. Daydreaming
O. Reacts violently to peer teasing
P. Sleeping in class
Q. Frequent crying

7. Inadequate parental discipline

A. Hyperactivity
B. Refuses to obey verbal instruction
C. Refuses to abide by rules.
D. Excessive crankiness
E. Excessive talking
F. Inability to retain verbal instructions
G. Physical violence
H. Lack of memory retention
I. Cannot stay on task
J. Handwriting impairment
K. Reading disability

L. Mathematics disability, cannot retain facts

M. Memorization impairment

N. Daydreaming

O. Reacts violently to peer teasing

P. Frequent crying

8. Sensitivity to preservatives

A. Hyperactivity

B. Excessive crankiness

C. Exhaustion

D. Excessive talking

E. Inability to retain verbal instructions

F. Physical violence

G. Lack of memory retention

H. Skin rashes

I. Asthma

J. Cannot stay on task

K. Recurring headaches

L. Handwriting impairment

M. Reading disability

N. Mathematics disability, cannot retain facts

O. Memorization impairment

P. Daydreaming

Q. Reacts violently to peer teasing

9. Poor classroom environment

A. Hyperactivity

B. Excessive crankiness

C. Exhaustion

D. Excessive talking

E. Inability to retain verbal instructions

F. Physical violence

G. Lack of memory retention

H. Cannot stay on task

I. Recurring headaches
J. Handwriting impairment
K. Reading disability
L. Mathematics disability, cannot retain facts
M. Memorization impairment
N. Daydreaming
O. Reacts violently to peer teasing

10. Family upheaval

A. Hyperactivity
B. Excessive crankiness
C. Exhaustion
D. Excessive talking
E. Inability to retain verbal instructions
F. Physical violence
G. Lack of memory retention
H. Stomach ache
I. Frequent crying
J. Cannot stay on task
K. Recurring headaches
L. Handwriting impairment
M. Reading disability
N. Mathematics disability, cannot retain facts
O. Memorization impairment
P. Daydreaming
Q. Reacts violently to peer teasing

It is interesting to note that many of the ADD symptoms cross over from one ADD trigger to the next. Hyperactivity is apparent in all categories. Based on this, it is imperative that the parent make sure that the child has been competently tested in all categories BEFORE the administration of behavior masking drugs. The child's problem could be as simple as a more challenging classroom environment, or a new pair of glasses.

The default for any child exhibiting hyperactivity is behavior-masking drugs. Almost 90% of the time the parent is guided toward the drugs by the school nurse, teacher or counselor.

In many cases the hyperactivity is caused by overcrowded classrooms. Thirty 7 -year-olds with one teacher and one teacher's assistant cannot maintain a calm nurturing environment. The teacher's time ends up making sure that the class does not explode on the ceiling. Teaching becomes a secondary activity.

In child care centers the rule of thumb for retaining some semblance of order is 6 to 8 (maximum) children per adult care giver. In consideration of this, how can we expect our children to have the best learning environment when the ratio is 16 up to 34 children to one adult?

In order to succeed in this environment the child needs to have strong scholastic guidance at home. The parent must interact daily, and help the child accomplish at night what it is impossible to accomplish in the current chaotic classroom environment. The parent must be a supplemental home teacher.

- 2 -
CAUSES OF ADD

There are many things to consider when diagnosing ADD (ADHD or ADLD). The following easily cured problems often disguise themselves as Attention Deficit Disorder. Before a child is given chemical intervention with behavior masking drugs, all the following hyperactivity triggers need to be tested and ruled out:

1. A diet full of sugar and caffeine.
2. Boredom due to high IQ
3. Learning-related visual impairment
4. Hearing impairment.
5. Hand to brain motor impairment.
6. Hypoglycemia and diabetes
7. Inadequate parental discipline
8. Sensitivity to preservatives
9. Poor classroom environment
10. Family upheaval

Children with either chemical or genetic imbalances will react strongly to categories #1 and #8. They will show classic symptoms of ADD (ADHD). The default treatment currently is to use behavior masking stimulant drugs such as Ritalin to suppress the symptoms rather than delete the trigger. This sets the child up for an explosion either from inadvertent drug withdrawal when medicine doses are not administered properly, or when the child builds up a resistance to the behavior masking drugs.

Like any other addiction, the sensitive child must be trained to ingest the proper, non-trigger foods, for the rest of his life. This sensitivity will ALWAYS be there. With guidance and proper nutrition the child can overcome the problem and live a normal productive life.

ADD SENSITIVITY TRIGGERS

1. A diet full of sugar and caffeine.

A child should not be put on drugs until all other possibilities have been ruled out. **Sugar and caffeine are the single most common triggers of ADD (ADHD & ADLD) behavior in children.** The first step in assessing a child's true behavior is to delete ALL sugar and caffeine from his diet. Some children can handle the additional glucose and stimulant in the system. Children that exhibit ADD symptoms many times are just suffering a negative drug reaction to personal overdoses of sugar and caffeine. When the child's system is CLEANED OUT, many times the ADD type behavior completely disappears. See case studies.

2. Boredom due to high IQ

Second most common false ADD symptom is the child who has an IQ level much more advanced than the curriculum being studied at his grade level in school. This causes boredom, and in many cases among bright children, misbehavior. The child's brain is not fully occupied, so they think of other activities to amuse themselves. Many times when a child is far ahead of his classmates mentally, he is taunted and called stupid. This is because the grade level classmates can't understand what the brighter child is talking about. His concepts are too advanced, and fly right over the other children's heads.

In this case the solution is to get the child into an appropriate curriculum, or home teach the child so he can move at a more aggressive academic pace. Children capable of absorbing great amounts of information quickly often show irritability in the classroom, and are impatient with the teacher when the teacher is forced to proceed at a pace more appropriate for the lowest common denominator in the classroom. See case studies.

3. Learning-related visual impairment

A visual impairment has been discovered that causes extreme discomfort when the affected individual is reading. The symptoms are extremely substandard reading scores, restive hyperactivity during reading periods, and reading with the head at an awkward angle. The affected child may score a perfect 20/20 on a regular vision test, and still seem to be almost incapable of learning to read. This can be assessed by administering the Comprehensive Learning Related Vision Exam. This exam tests eye movement control, focusing near to far, sustaining clear focus, eye teaming ability, depth perception, visual motor interaction, form perception and visual memory.

The good news is that children that have this problem are easily helped and in many cases have jumped two to four reading grade levels immediately as well as ceasing the misbehavior during reading time. They can go from problem child to brilliant almost overnight. See case studies.

4. Hearing impairment.

In spite of the fact that hearing impairment is such an obvious cause of Attention Deficit Disorder, many times it is overlooked. The child may be masking his disability well. Generally the child will be accused of not listening or paying attention in class. For the child with the hearing disorder it is too much effort to hear the teacher over all the ambient noise of a crowded classroom. A hearing test is a must for all children thought to be ADD. The proper hearing aid, and/or special education class is an immediate cure for this problem. See case studies.

5. Hand to brain motor impairment.

There is a rarely diagnosed, but common, disability that causes the signal to become garbled between a child's hand and his brain. The prime symptom also is considered a prime symptom of ADD. It is bad handwriting. The child grips the pencil desperately, awkwardly forming the letters, only to leave out whole words from his sentences. The parent of this child is told his child is lazy.

Testing for this motor control disability can be administered along with the rest of the tests used by resource specialists to diagnose ADD (ADHD). Many times however it is not included. A parent must insist on it. The child that does have this synapse disconnection will fly forward in accomplishment if allowed to work on computer. On computer he does not have to construct the letters, he merely has to hit the key. This is an immediate F to an A+ in many cases. See case studies.

6. Hypoglycemia and diabetes

Here are two of very common causes of ADD-type behavior. The child's body cannot deal with the amount of sugar in his system. He will experience highs just after eating and then severe lows. Sometimes, in the case of diabetes, the child will sleep incessantly or pass out from sugar consumption after meals.

The child will not be able to control his emotions, crying over trivial matters at a much later age than his peers. Frequently this child is labeled a cry-baby. If the child's system is sensitive to sugar, whether due to a chemical disorder in the front of his brain or a genetic burp on the chromosome string, the child MUST be given an altered dietary intake. The system must be cleaned out and the parents must be very vigilant when shopping to see that the child does not ingest any foods that are double loaded with sugar.

The child should also be allowed more small meals rather than three large meals a day. This will help to stabilize his frail system.

The diabetic child must be diagnosed and receive the proper medical care. A borderline diabetic will not show the severe symptoms of the more classic diabetic. Diabetes and hyperglycemia are often misdiagnosed as ADD.

Proper diagnosis, trigger identification, is a much preferable solution than putting a child on behavior masking drugs that will stifle his appetite, stunt his growth and cause him to behave like a zombie. The diabetes or hypoglycemia will still be there, and in spite of the behavior masking drugs, eventually rear it's cataclysmic head. Then the cure might be much more difficult than an early diagnosis.

The detox from the behavior masking drugs is harsh. Children have gone berserk as they build up resistance to the drugs. They continually need higher and higher doses. There have been cases of children in Ritalin withdrawal stabbing others in the classroom with scissors and/or having to be hospitalized. Is this the right solution when the child could be virtually cured by simple changes in his or her diet or education?

7. Inadequate Parental Discipline

In this day of academic disciplinary restraint, many times the only course open to a school to solve the problem of a school bully or troublemaker is to try to get the child moved onto a behavior masking drug such as Ritalin. The school justifies the detriment of turning one child into a zombie for the greater good of the rest of the students.

The parent has to fairly assess his in home discipline. If the child ignores "no" at home, then he also will at school. If the child is noisy and ill behaved at the supermarket, if the parent has no control, nor will the school.

The parent must decide if they want to drug their child, or are willing to enter into some discipline parenting seminars in order to correct the discipline problem. See case studies.

Often the root cause of a child diagnosed with ADD (ADHD) is lack of parental discipline. This is usually a parent who says no to a child, but changes it to yes if the child screams or behaves in an irrational manner. These parents are usually afraid of the scene their child is making, and give in to quiet the child to save face with onlookers. Unfortunately, early on a child realizes he can get anything he wants by making a scene. Essentially, the parent has taught his child to scream. This behavior is completely unacceptable in the school environment. The school, however, has little or no recourse against a child used to getting his way at all costs. Many times the solution for the school is to try to get the child on a behavior masking drug. This calms him down in the classroom, and allows the other children around him to learn.

Each parent knows in their heart whether "No is No" or if they allow their child win by misbehavior. The deprogramming is not pleasant, but can be accomplished with a good support group of parents and grand parents.

This deprogramming is imperative in order to give the child the tools he will need to succeed in the real world.

8. Sensitivity to preservatives

This sensitivity usually goes hand in hand with sugar and caffeine sensitivity. There is a comprehensive test that can be given to identify all the substances that a child's body reacts to. If diagnosed with preservative sensitivity the parent has a choice. Get all the offending foods out of the home, and detox the child, or put the child on a behavior masking drug such as Ritalin. The best way to heal the child is to delete the offending foods.

9. Poor classroom environment

Most teachers are well trained and passionate about their careers. otherwise they would not be teachers. Unfortunately sometimes a teacher is unable to maintain order in n overcrowded classroom, and the quality of teaching suffers. Young children do very poorly in a learning environment that is chaotic. Due to a lack of adequate discipline recourse, there is also much more verbally abusive language and actions in the classroom today than in the past. If a child is showing poor performance at school, the parent should sit in on some classes and judge for themselves if they feel their child is in a truly nurturing learning environment, or merely trapped for six to eight hours in chaos.

10. Family upheaval

When a family goes through a traumatic experience such as death or divorce, it is not uncommon for a child to misbehave. This is an expression of his grief. At this time the child needs psychological support, not behavior masking drugs. Usually when the dust settles the child, if properly nurtured, will resume his older behavior.

Many time the parents trigger the misbehavior by venting their anger at a departing spouse on the child. The child passes on that anger on the school yard. It's unfortunate that in many divorces the children are used as sounding boards for both parent's anger with the other, items that they are not psychologically strong enough to absorb or process.

In summary, many times it's easier for the school to encourage the parent to put the child on ADD behavior masking medication, than to address whatever is the root of the child's misbehavior problem. If a child is bringing candy bars to school in his lunch, and subsequently freaking out in fourth period, the school has to take action. If the parents and the school don't see the connection between the candy bars eaten at lunch and the misbehavior, or if the parents refuse to delete the offending sugar, the child may be misdiagnosed as ADD by the school out of defense for the other students. Many times it's easier to cave in and just drug the child than to take the child off his current drug, the candy.

- 3 -

WHICH CAME FIRST— THE CHICKEN OR THE EGG?

All parents who have a sensitive (ADD) child, at some time wonder why there seem to be so many affected children now. In 1995 some statistics showed that over ten percent of elementary school children were on the drug Ritalin. According to the United States Government Office of Mental Health at least two million children have been diagnosed as having ADD/ADHD. Because ADLD is so inert, and does not cause conflict, the statistics on this aspect of the ADD syndrome is not available at this time. As more people become aware of ADLD, there will be more data available.

Older parents remember a time when there were only one or two troublemakers in the whole school. Also, coincidentally, there was usually only one or two fat kids. Now there is at least one diagnosed ADD/ADHD child PER CLASS, and overweight children in some schools account for as much as 50 to 75% of the student body.

There is a trend among physicians to move adults onto behavior-masking drugs, much to the delight of the Eli Lilly Corporation, the manufacturer of the behavior-masking drug Ritalin.

The number of children sensitive to sugar and preservatives hasn't changed over the years, the access has. Thanks to Madison Avenue, every minute a child watches TV he is being assailed with advertisements for sugary cereals, candy bars and other sugary snack food ads. Moms no longer cook good foods from scratch. Healthy vegetables are not brought in from the garden. We troll through the freezer and canned foods for our meals. Many fast foods are preserved with sugar, such as pizza, ravioli and spaghetti sauces.

In the grocery store a responsible mom has to diligently search out the breakfast cereals that are not constructed like a sugary dessert, and find those with actual nutritional value. The primary grocery shopper in the family has to train herself or himself to recognize such terms as "high fructose' and "corn syrup" as exactly what they are, types of sugars. High fructose actually has more power than regular refined sugar, while the common misconception is that it's not as bad as sugar. It's actually two to three times worse as an ADD trigger. Honey as well, because it's a natural substance, is often mistaken as an appropriate replacement for sugar, when in fact it's equal in destructive power to an ADD sensitive.

With dual working parents, many children are making their own meals, sometimes making meals for the entire family. It's not surprising that the meals are heavy on the sugar or sugar producing starches, and light on the vegetables, protein and calcium.

In fast food restaurants milk is so seldom ordered by parents for their children that there have been incidents where new counter help has to ask the management if it's OK to exchange milk for the soda pop.

In this climate of massive sugar abuse it's no wonder children are being diagnosed as hyperactive dysfunctionals. The good news is that many of these children can be completely cured.

- 4 -
DIAGNOSING THE PROBLEM

Most commonly it is the school who informs the parent that their child may be ADD (ADHD). Prior to going to school a child is allowed to play freely, and unless the problem is severe, it is generally not noticed until the child is required to function in a more structured environment.

Commonly the parent will get a phone call from school for a conference. During the conference the parent will be informed that the school fears the child is suffering from ADD (ADHD) Syndrome, and should see a doctor and/or a therapist for help. Many times a parent is told forcefully by the school that the child HAS ADD even though no tests have been administered to the child. In sad cases the parent accepts the school's judgment meekly, and submits his child to chemical therapy without any other corroborative testing.

During the meeting at school the parent will be told horror stories recounting the child's severe misbehavior in class or on the play yard. The parent will feel embarrassed and ashamed. They will want to stop the bad behavior as quickly as possible, so they will not be perceived as BAD PARENTS. It is not surprising that the parents agree to drug their children with no further testing. They want to solve the problem at school as quickly as possible and to regain their face as good parents.

When the parent is confronted by the accusing phalanx of teacher, Principle, school nurse and counselor, the most understandable reaction is shame that their child is causing problems. The parent experiences immediate guilt that they are somehow inadequate parents, or their child is a bad child.

Neither case is likely to be true (although admittedly there are bad parents). Because the ADD syndrome is caused by either a chemical or genetic imbalance in the child's brain or other ADD triggers such as vision impairment or high IQ, the child is not in control. Neither is the parent. The child is suffering an ongoing natural reaction to these triggers causing him to behave outside of the accepted norm.

In order to fix the problem, the trigger needs to be identified and the child needs to be stabilized by deleting the trigger. When this is accomplished the magical metamorphosis takes place and the child moves from ADD-impaired to excellent.

At the time of the cataclysmic school conference the parent has choices. Immediately, BEFORE the child is given ANY behavior masking drug therapy, the parent needs to insist the child be administered tests by the school to assess his behavior. THIS IS THE PARENT'S RIGHT BY LAW IN MOST STATES.

The parent needs to ask for a comprehensive IEP evaluation. The parent does not want to take the word of just casual classroom observation, there are specific tests that can be administered that will assess if the child truly has the genetic or chemical ADD imbalance, or if the problem is merely high IQ and extreme boredom. High IQ is a frequent masquerader as ADD. Sadly, many potential Einsteins are wasting away as drooling zombies on behavior-masking drugs. They will never reach their full potential merely for the lack of adequate diagnostic testing.

Too many times an embarrassed and chagrined parent trots obediently off to the doctor, and has his child put on stimulants such as Ritalin. In sad cases this will permanently derail a prospective Einstein.

Stimulants are very hard on a child's system. They cause loss of appetite and stunt the growth. The body builds up a resistance and the child may need escalating medication. Before inflicting this on your child, you MUST assess whether this is actually necessary. Is it right for your child, or merely a quick and convenient (and expensive) way to solve a dietary, discipline or attention problem in the classroom?

After the school has administered the battery of IEP tests they will know if Johnny is suffering from overly developed IQ (See Case Study #4) or actual ADD syndrome. They will be able to tell the parent unequivocally if the child can focus when interested in a task, or is incapable of focus. This is a very crucial piece of information, because a bright, bored child should not be thrown on behavior masking drugs for the convenience of those around him.

The IEP tests should not be administered by the on-premises school personnel such as the child's teacher, principle, nurse or counselor, as that often contributes bias to the testing. It should be administered by a Special Education or Resource Counselor trained specifically in this area. She will have no bias with the child.

Should you have a positive diagnosis by the resource specialist that there is a real Attention Deficit Disorder, the parent's next stop is the child's physician. The parent needs to rule out hyperglycemia, diabetes, vision and hearing and other medical problems that may be causing the syndrome that can be medically managed.

If there is no clear medical evidence of diabetes or other physical disorder, the next action is to take the child to Ground Zero. This means deleting all foods from the child's diet that are ADD triggers. Once a parent has taken the child to Ground Zero a true assessment can be made of the medical needs of the child.

Another thing that must be considered at this time is the family situation. There are children who react to divorce or other family stress by exhibiting the symptoms of ADD. They don't need behavior masking drugs, they need caring therapy, maybe also a "big brother or "big sister" to help them through the tough psychological transition of divorce.

Many children who have brain sensitivity to certain foods or preservatives (whether chemical or genetic) can be virtually cured of ADD Syndrome by careful diet. This is a much preferable solution to drugging the child to mask the problem. A careful Ground Zero diet will not only cure the misbehavior, but assist the child in developing normal health, weight and brain development. These areas are hindered by the administration of behavior masking drugs.

Going to Ground Zero with a child can be a temporarily wearing process, but the rewards are a healthy, happy well adjusted productive child.

- 5 -
CASE STUDIES

Before we get into Ground Zero procedures here are interesting case studies of children and adults thought to suffer from ADD (ADHD or ADLD). You may find a description of your own child here, or even yourself. The names have been changed to protect the privacy of the families studied.

Different individuals have different tolerance levels to sugar and caffeine. Just as some people can overeat with no adverse weight gain, so can others ingest large amounts of sugar or caffeine with no adverse side effects. The following case studies are of individuals who react to sometimes infinitesimal amounts of sugar or caffeine. It must be remembered that they are not bad. They are having a bad reaction to readily available household drugs—sugar and caffeine.

Case Study #1.1
A diet full of sugar and caffeine.
ADLD - The Author's Story

I came from a very well educated household. My parents were college graduates in highly technical careers. My brothers and sister and I tested highly on IQ tests.

None of the children in our family could focus in school. I was very hyperactive. When forced to buckle down, finish something, I threw a tantrum. I wanted to move on. When forced to sit still for meals my body would vibrate with repetitive motion. My foot would tap incessantly under the table. I constantly was in hot water with my parents for shaking my knee under the table.

I also suffered from chronic constipation, painful bowel movements. I remember long painful bouts in the bathroom very early. In school I would make origami boats out of the small tissue squares in the bathroom while waiting incessantly for a bowel movement.

In our house the day started with either a bowl of cereal covered with sugar, or pancakes drowning in syrup. Before I was school age my mother would buy all her children cream puffs off the ice cream truck. Mother also specialized in wonderful homemade donuts and other pastries. A favorite household snack was cinnamon toast—warm toast with butter, sprinkled with a thick layer of sugar and cinnamon.

We were encouraged to drink our milk by mixing in sugar and chocolate. Every night a sweet dessert was served after dinner. We were bribed to clean our plates in order to get the dessert. My father has said it took hours for my sister and I to finish our dinners. "We had to practically force feed you," he stated.

When the family went out to eat we were encouraged to eat the sugar cubes on the dinner table until our meal arrived.

In high school I was in severe sugar addiction. I also started drinking caffeine laced soda pop. In my first class period I would suffer the sugar low following the sugar high of breakfast. I could not concentrate. I could not spell, could not retain even the simplest math concepts. I excelled in drama as a character actress, but could never remember the lines to my scripts. I learned to fake it.

After second period at school, I would buy a sweet

roll from the school snack bar. In third period, I could barely keep my eyes open. My body was on an extreme overload from sugar. I fought to stay awake. I could not follow anything the teacher was saying. I would daydream. I was not able to focus or answer even a simple question. I would almost pass out.

At lunch I would eat the full cafeteria meal followed by cake with icing. In fourth period, I would fall asleep with my head in my hands, many times awaking to find myself drooling. After school, I would have one or two caffeine laced soda pops.

At home, I did not enjoy physical activities. I wanted to read or sleep most of the time. I was constantly exhausted. Regularly before dinner, or at dinner, I would fly into verbally abusive rages for no apparent reason. I remember feeling paralyzing anger for no reason. I had no close friends.

At Christmas time, the family was always given a huge box of chocolates by one of my father's clients. I would sneak into the closet where the candy was hidden and eat piece after piece. The candy would scream at me until it was all gone. If it was in the house, I had to have it.

After leaving home my diet consisted of Twinkies, Coke and lemonade. I was completely unfocused, unable to concentrate. I was hyper and continually moving from place to place, project to project. My caffeine addiction grew worse. On the days I did not drink the caffeine laced soda pop I would suffer paralyzing withdrawal headaches. I lived on Excedrin (containing caffeine). My constipation got worse, and I started suffering from recurring vaginitis.

At 30 years of age I started dating a man who did not eat sugar. The first time I served cereal the way he wanted it, plain granola with only milk, I gagged on it. To me the taste, without the sugar, was completely foreign. All my life food had been merely a canvas for sugar. My addiction to sugar was monstrous.

In consideration of the fact I wanted to spend time with this man, and had to cook for him, I found myself detoxing from the sugar. An acquaintance talked me into doing a two week fast to clean out my system. (See chapter 33 on Detox Fasting.) Once I removed all the built up debris from my lower intestine, my vaginitis disappeared. I moved to a no sugar, high fiber diet and have been vaginitis-free ever since. Once I was off sugar, my painful, lifelong constipation also completely disappeared.

For the first time in my life, I found myself able to focus for long periods of time on one thing. I took up the computer, which I had never had the patience to learn before. Seemingly overnight, I went from hyperactive to focused. In the next three years I accomplished more than I had in the previous 33. I became a prolific writer. I learned to spell. I no longer suffered from chronic constipation, vaginitis or headaches. I now go for years at a time with no aspirin or Excedrin in the house. The exhaustion also went away. I no longer required the excessive amount of sleep and I wake up easily in the morning. At 40 years old, due to excess breast lumps, I decided to quit the caffeine.

To this day, I feel rage that a thing as simple as sugar in my diet kept me from fulfilling my potential. As a child I wanted to be an architect, but I could not focus in class. I wanted to be a photographer, but I could never remember to set the F-stop or take a light reading. I wanted to be an actress, but I could not remember the lines. I wanted to be a musician, but I could never sit still long enough to practice.

In the eighteen years since detoxing I have written title songs for films and television, recorded an album, produced many bands in the studio, patented three extremely complex photographic inventions which required years of research. I have written three novels, four scripts and two nonfiction books.

The cure for my ADLD was not to mask it with drugs, but to delete the root cause, the triggers, which is a much cheaper and more productive cure. The cure gave me back myself, and let me fulfill virtually every dream I had as a child. Soon my son and I will build a house of our own design, another one of my dreams.

Every day I fight my addiction to sugar and caffeine. I will never be over my craving for it. Some days I fall off the wagon, and pay the price, but I can stand outside of myself and attempt to control the rage and irrationality that comes with the sugar high.

I still have difficulty balancing my checkbook so I have a business manager who tries to keep me out of trouble. I have accepted my disability, and I try to accommodate it's requirements.

Most of all I'm glad to have been rescued at 30.

Case Study #1.2
A diet full of sugar and caffeine - ADHD

Jenny was diagnosed by school and doctor as ADD. She was put on a regimen of Ritalin. Her moods were very volatile—very high ups and deep downs. When she wasn't on drug therapy, she would talk and fidget incessantly and have violent screaming tantrums. When she was on the behavior-masking drug, she lost her appetite and refused to eat.

As a teenager, she was still throwing tearful kicking tantrums that caused her to be a pariah among more functional children her age. She spoke very abusively to those around her when she was in one of her moods. She could not absorb a simple instruction unless she was yelled at severely. She was verbally abusive to other children. Everyone but her family avoided being around her she was so disruptive. She had no friends at school.

The parents stated that Jenny was just like her father. They felt that the ADD plus the temper was inherited from him. The parents were desperate for a solution. They felt Jenny's chemical therapy was the answer.

In researching the dietary habits of the household, it turned out that in fact Jenny WAS just like her father. She definitely had inherited his eating patterns. They both preferred to eat sweets rather than meals. There were bowls full of candy bars around the house. The father kept bags of candy bars handy. Jenny was allowed to eat ice cream and drink coke in place of real food for lunch. It was no wonder her behavior was so erratic and extreme. She was two inches away from diabetes as well. She had to urinate constantly, and was grossly undersized. At 13-years-old, Jenny was the size and temperament of an 8-year-old.

When questioned about why they let Jenny eat ice cream instead of real food, the parents said that Jenny's pediatrician had suggested it because she had so little appetite on the behavior-masking Ritalin that she needed any food she would eat. Jenny had learned that she could eat whatever she liked by simply saying "I'm not hungry" and refusing real food. It is remarkable that the pediatrician did not know that contemporary ice cream not only has absolutely no nutritive value, but kills off all the valuable enzymes in the intestine as it travels through the bowels. This was the worst thing Jenny could do to herself.

After studying the eating habits of the family it was clear what was causing Jenny's ADD, as well as her father's. There was an extraordinary high ingestion of sugar and caffeine in the household.

The first job was to remove all ADD trigger foods from the house. This included not only the candy bars, but the frosted cereals, donuts, ice cream, popsicles, soda pop, and cookies. Many crackers turn directly to sugar in the blood stream. For that reason many diabetics are advised to keep saltine crackers around in case of a crash. Jenny's parents were encouraged to keep a dietary log so they could track the sugar intake. The parents refused. They could not see the harm in their diet.

We did manage to isolate Jenny for long periods at a time. Instead of eating ice cream and Coke for lunch, Jenny was given foods such as plain grilled chicken sandwiches and milk. At first Jenny refused the foods, her choice for lunch was chocolate cake and a milk shake, or two apple pies and a Coke. "My mom lets me." We refused to give her these items.

Inevitably she got hungry and started to eat the good food we had provided. That afternoon Jenny was able to concentrate. She did her homework without being told to. Afterward she played quietly listening to CDs. Her speech patterns were normal, and she could grasp instructions immediately instead of having to be yelled at. Her highs were much lower and lows were much higher. Her "magical metamorphosis" had happened.

Her behavior was an amazing example of Jeckel and Hyde. Fed a no-sugar, high-calcium diet Jenny was calm, could understand verbal instruction and quietly entertained herself. She was also easily able to go two hours and more between bathroom stops. The frequent urination was not in evidence.

In contrast, the next time we spent time with Jenny she was taken on a car trip. The drink provided to her by her parent for the trip was a sports bottle of low dilution Tang (sugar and water). She was unfocused, talked loudly, incessantly. Jenny could not remember even the most basic verbal instruction more that a few minutes at a time at best.

It isn't easy for Jenny. She will always crave sugar

just like an alcoholic will always crave a drink. She has to confront the fact that her father insists that bowls of candy bars be available to him. The default drink for her is Coke, not milk. But she can feel the difference at Ground Zero. The times we've controlled her diet she feels the change and talks to us about it.

Like an alcoholic, she has her good days and her bad days. It would be easier for Jenny if her family could acknowledge their addiction to sugar and caffeine, and also go to Ground Zero. It would be easier if her mother did not offer her sugary treats to get her ready for some unpleasant task, feeding her addiction. It would be easier on Jenny if they could keep proper foods in the house. This makes it much easier for the affected members to avoid the foods they can't eat. It's also much healthier for the entire family.

Jenny's parents made the decision to continue Jenny on the behavior masking drugs. They are unwilling to change her diet.

Jenny is growing up. Hopefully, when she is old enough to control her diet she will remember the information we've given her. Hopefully she will choose to eat properly.

When she falls off the wagon, she can stand back and assess that her irrational misbehavior has been triggered by a chemical reaction in her brain caused by sugar or caffeine intake. She can take steps to isolate herself until she can stabilize her behavior. Hopefully she will start to take charge of her machine. Hopefully she will remember the lessons we've taught her when she is on her own.

Most importantly Jenny now knows she's not a bad kid. She's just sensitive to certain foods. When she grows up and leaves home she will have the opportunity to put this knowledge to work and clean up her dietary lifestyle, and to be reborn to a healthier lifestyle.

Case Study #1.3
A diet full of sugar - ADHD

Trent was a very interesting case. Upon observing him, the initial opinion was that he was just raised completely without discipline. His parents were divorced. His mother, whom he lived with, was very focused on her career, and Trent seemed to be a rudderless boat on the water. Trent was oversized, and regularly beat up littler kids. On one occasion he was observed to bruisingly strike his father with no repercussion whatsoever.

He was not exhibiting the severe hyperactivity in our presence that is most traditionally connected to sugar sensitivity. Mainly he was just a behaving as a rude bully.

Years later we ran into an acquaintance of Trent's and asked how he was.

"You know," said the acquaintance, "Trent's mom finally took him off sugar. He was at a pancake house one day and he started out fine—well-behaved and quiet. Shortly after eating a plate of pancakes covered in syrup, he started beating his head repetitively against the back of the booth. He went crazy. It was amazing, scary. That finally convinced his mother that it was the sugar causing his violent behavior. She sat right there and watched it happen in front of her eyes, just like a movie. The sugar hit him like a truck."

Case Study #1.4
A Diet Full Of Sugar - ADHD

Jimmy grew up before ADD was identified. He was raised by a mother predisposed to alcoholism. Because his mother craved sugar, Jimmy's diet was full of donuts, chocolate milk,and cookies. Jimmy couldn't focus for more than a few moments at a time. His temperament was extremely erratic. He vacillated from a state of cheerful euphoria to violent anger and verbal abuse.

His mother and father would make him clean his plate using the dessert as a bribe. They felt if he didn't clean his plate they were not being good responsible parents. This doubled his problems by force feeding him when he was the best judge of his capacity and needs. Now a full grown adult with a low metabolism, Jimmy continually fights obesity.

Two of Jimmy's siblings never had problems with appetite, they would shovel down the food. To this day they are slender, with high metabolisms. There's a message here, if a child desires small amounts of food, but is in good health and weight, he may not need to eat the same volume as other siblings with higher metabolisms. As long as the foods the child has available are nutritious, let the child be the judge of what they need.

Years later, tired of the constant yo-yo dieting Jimmy started eating "Ground Zero" meals. For the first time, Jimmy felt normal. With the diet change came the ability to focus. Overnight Jimmy changed from a talker to a doer. For the first time in his life he could wake up in the morning refreshed with a clear head. Within two years Jimmy had accomplished more than in his entire previous adult life.

Jimmy has to struggle daily with his addiction to sugar and food. Now that he knows the source of the problem, that it isn't he who is bad, he's able to cope. Some days the anger at his parents for the food and sugar they shoveled down him is overwhelming. Most of the time he can rationally tell himself that his parents weren't wrong, they were just misinformed. Everything they did for him was out of their love for him and their perceived responsibility to make him eat right.

It's sad that Jimmy was so affected by something as simple to correct as diet. Today Jimmy watches what he eats carefully, and is raising his children at Ground Zero. Jimmy knows there is a very high percentage chance that his children suffer the same sugar sensitivity, and slow metabolism as he, and he's taking no chances. All of Jimmy's siblings have, late in life, corrected their eating disorders. Like reformed smokers, they are vigilant advocates of the Ground Zero diet.

Case Study #2.1
Boredom Due to High IQ - ADHD
Robbie's Story

Robbie's mother was called to school. She was told that Robbie couldn't concentrate. He was not turning in his work and he couldn't focus. His handwriting was years behind the other children in his class. The school told the mother that Robbie was ADD. They insisted that Robbie's mother contact his pediatrician and ask for medical help.

Robbie's pediatrician told his mother that never in the seven years that Robbie had been her patient had she ever seen any indication that Robbie suffered from ADD. To her he seemed extremely focused and attentive. The pediatrician insisted that the mother ask for comprehensive testing by the school district's resource department before she would consider chemical intervention.

The mother requested the testing. Robbie was given a two week long battery of tests. The tests proved conclusively that Robbie could concentrate when he wished to do so. His scores were very high. In virtually all subjects he was years ahead of his second grade classmates. The result of the testing was that Robbie could take two years off from school if he wished and would not suffer scholastically.

Robbie's misbehavior in class was due to boredom, lack of mental stimulation. Because he grasps concepts so much quicker than the other children he tends to focus on every little event, thereby causing him to loose task focus and be disruptive. He tends to ask questions that the teacher many times feels totally irrelevant to the subject at hand. He was moved to an accelerated scholastic program, and put into the Gifted and Talented Education Program.

Several years later in fourth grade when Robbie moved to a different school district he was tested again. This time his reading and vocabulary level was college grade 16. In all areas but one he was still way ahead.

Bright children must be moved at a faster pace, not subdued with drugs. This is not sometimes the convenient route, the parent may have to scream like crazy to get the proper accommodations for his child. The parent may have to home school the child to allow him to move at a highly accelerated rate. The alternative, behavior masking chemical therapy is is a criminal cure for a bright bored child in the classroom. Do we want to turn a potential Einstein into a drugged zombie?

Case Study #3.1
Learning Related Visual Impairment
Learning Disabled/ADD

When John was a child he couldn't read. His parents had been told he had a learning disability. He must be put into special education classes where the challenged children were able to work at their own pace. His parents, knowing that he was bright, not believing he was learning disabled, took him to specialist after specialist. John was given eye tests, he had 20/20 vision. He was given hearing tests, he had perfect hearing. Finally they decided to put him into a special private school.

One day they gave John a brand new bike. John couldn't ride it. Every time he tried he fell over. His parents watched him try time and time again. They noticed that when he was attempting to ride, he held his head at an awkward angle. He held his head to the side, and looked out of the corner of his eyes. His parents told him to point his head straight forward. They figured that the awkward head angle was throwing off his balance. John told them he couldn't hold his head straight forward. When he looked straight ahead he saw two of everything.

John's parents were shocked. They had stumbled over a vision problem that had not been diagnosed by the many expensive specialists they had taken him to.This was something that all previous medical talent had missed completely.

A parent at John's private school suggested they take him to see learning related vision pioneer Orthoptic Optetrician Dr. Joseph Katz in Northbrook, Illinois. They rushed him over.

Dr. Katz gave John a Comprehensive Learning Related Visual Exam. It was immediately apparent that John's eyes were not working properly together in spite of the fact that each eye was functioning well on it's own. Dr. Katz prescribed stress relieving glasses for John, and immediately John went from a learning disabled to an excellent student. His reading level jumped several grades at a time quickly, and he became an avid reader. Today he is a successful commercial photographer.

Both of John's younger brothers were born with the same vision related learning disorder, but the parents were aware, and looking for it. They had diagnosed and corrected it before the subsequent children started to read.

John's mother, Ann Schulz, has been the Director of The Coast Kids Theatre Company in Encinitas, California for the last fifteen years. "Many times I've seen a child with the same problem in my children's theatre group," States Mrs. Schulz, "I'm so happy I can steer the parent to the right solution for their child, there is currently so little awareness of this visual impairment. Many children are being diagnosed as learning impaired, or ADD when in fact, they just need the proper glasses and a few exercises to excel."

Case Study #4.1
Hearing Impairment - ADHD

Tommy was a nightmare in class. He was loud and disruptive. He talked incessantly during class. He never "paid attention". The other children called him stupid because he never knew the proper answers to the teacher's questions. He would fight in and out of the classroom, exploding back at the children who taunted him. The school called in the parents. They told them that Tommy had a severe learning disability, was ADD and needed chemical therapy and psychological help.

Tommy definitely needed psychological help, but his problem was as simple as a hearing aid and proper seating. When the parents called the family physician to diagnose ADD behavior masking drugs the pediatrician refused. She told the parents to demand the testing that would be provided by the district's resource department free of charge. The pediatrician said that if he truly tested ADD And learning disabled, she would refer him for more tests. Only when she was completely convinced that his disorder was not addressable any other way would the pediatrician agree to administer behavior drugs to Tommy.

Tommy's tests included a simple hearing exam. His hearing showed up as severely impaired. It had not been previously diagnosed because Tommy spoke properly, although loudly. He did not show the traditional symptoms of hearing impairment. So he had not been tested.

Tommy was moved to the front of the class with his

good ear facing the teacher, and provided with a hearing aid. His behavior turned around immediately. He was a bright interested boy when he could hear the teacher. His grades soared.

If it hadn't been for that knowledgeable pediatrician, Tommy would be on chemical therapy today, he would be in a SED classroom filled with dysfunctional and violent children. Instead Tommy is now at the top of his class, a productive member of his school, making his parents proud.

Case Study #5.1
Hand to Brain Motor Impairment. - ADHD

Timmy was diagnosed by the experts at his school as being ADD. When tested it proved that although extremely bright, Timmy could not process brain to hand. He had a synapse block that made it extremely difficult for him to write or draw by hand. He had to concentrate so hard just getting the forms of the letters on the paper that he would leave out words or letters and have to start over. His handwriting was years behind and stagnate. No matter how much practice he did, it did not improve. Homework that would take other children thirty minutes would take Timmy hours to complete properly.

The IEP tests indicated that he would excel even more rapidly if he was allowed to use a computer rather than be required to write by hand. With a computer he had merely to hit a key rather than construct visual images of the letters. This his brain could handle with ease.

In spite of this disability, Timmy still scored 139 on his IQ test. This is extremely high considering that the substandard scores in written/oral dictation and handwriting brought his IQ average measurably lower than it actually was.

The parents were relieved. At the previous school

Timmy had often tried to turn in assignments done on the family's computer, only to be told he had to write them by hand to perfect his substandard writing skills. He would struggle tearfully for hours trying to get the words to paper. He also suffered self esteem damage when told he wasn't trying hard enough to write properly.

After working with Timmy's ADHD , his written assignments went from substandard to A+.

Case Study #6.1
Hypoglycemia and Diabetes. - ADHD

Emilia suffered extremely deep bouts of depression and very euphoric highs. She was hyperactive. Talked incessantly. When she hit a low, she would completely lose focus. As an adult she had frequent minor accidents from lack of attention to the road.

During her conversations she would vector abruptly from one subject to another without seguey or preamble. Although it was long before ADD had become a trendy catch all for various chemical imbalances, Emilia was a classic case of ADD (ADHD).

In spite of her dysfunction, Emilia was brilliant. She absorbed an amazing amount of information and was knowledgeable on many different subjects. Her few passionate friends learned to translate her dialog, and follow her conversation wherever it would ramble.

Finally, after years of dysfunction Emilia was diagnosed as hypoglycemic. She started eating many small meals throughout the day rather than large meals three times a day. Emilia also cut processed sugar completely out of her diet.

Due to extraordinarily high IQ, it still took complete attention to follow her conversations, but her high mood swings and lack of focus calmed down.

Hypoglycemia and diabetes must be tested in children accused of ADD or misbehavior. The mood swings can be cured simply with proper diet and the administration of insulin for the diabetic.

In the case of diabetes, severe cases are usually diagnosed because the child will slip into a coma if he does not eat properly. In mild cases it can go undiscovered as the child is derided for improper behavior.

If your child has been tentatively diagnosed with ADD (ADHD) a glucose tolerance test is imperative to rule out the possibility of diabetes or hypoglycemia.

Case Study #7.1
Inadequate Parental Discipline - ADHD

Bobbie would not stay in his seat in kindergarten. He would drop to the floor and pound his feet when asked to do an unpleasant task. He was a nightmare at school. On the schoolyard he would have screaming tantrums if a child tried to play where he wanted to play, or wanted him to share. The word no was meaningless. He had to be physically sequestered when in time out.

Bobbie's ADHD was created by his parents. They, admittedly, had never trained him to accept no for an answer. If he wanted something all he had to do was throw a tantrum and the desired object was his. His parents thought giving him this freedom was showing him love. They were afraid if they denied him that he would not love them anymore.

Bobbie had trained his parents well. Unfortunately, when he went to school, this technique didn't work. Bobbie's parents had set him up for abysmal failure. He was treated like an outcast by both his peers and teachers.

Bobbie's parents decided to apply proper and consistent discipline. They wanted to train their child for success, and they knew the only way to do it was to de program his inappropriate behavior.

The first application was very traumatic. Bobbie screamed for an hour when denied his usual second dessert after dinner. He screamed that he hated his parents. He threw his dinner dishes to the floor.

His parents ignored his behavior and stuck to their guns. They felt miserable. They were sure Bobbie would hate them for the rest of their life. Finally they put a still screaming child into bed. He eventually, exhausted, dropped off to sleep.

The next day Bobbie again threw a tantrum. This time it was in the supermarket. Bobbie's mom had an adrenalin rush. Her first instinct was to give Bobbie the requested item to quiet him as quickly as possible. Instead she stuck to her no, and, extremely embarrassed, dragged Bobbie, screaming, from the store. This time the screaming lasted for a half hour and then subsided.

The third time Bobbie only displayed his tantrum for ten gruesome minutes. The next time his mother said no, he accepted it. He knew that she would not change her mind.

Consistently Bobbie tries the screaming approach with every new care giver or educator. Those that he can manipulate in this way he does.Bobbie's grandparents still are embarrassed by him in public, because they cannot bring themselves to stick to no. They are creating their own nightmare. Those that don't buy it see a very different Bobbie—one that behaves well and takes no for an answer.

Case Study #8.1
Sensitivity To Preservatives - ADHD

Jenny was not consistent with her ADD misbehavior. She would go for long periods of time perfectly fine, and then out of the blue behave hyperactively. When this behavior struck she would not be able to grasp the simplest instruction, not be able to sit still. She would talk incessantly.

Originally diagnosed as ADD, Jenny was given behavior masking drugs. Eventually, through allergy testing, it proved that she was allergic to red dye and wheat. Once these items were deleted from her diet Jenny became a consistently normally functioning child.

Case Study 9.1
A Fracture in the Family—ADHD/ADLD

Paulie's parents were constantly being called by the school due to his misbehavior. The parents finally decided that Ritalin was the best option.

Unconsidered at the time was the brutal divorce the parents were undergoing. Paulie was psychologically pulled limb from limb by the parents. He was subjected to hours of abusive ranting by each parent about the other. It was no wonder he was dishing it out at school. He was in severe distress.

The decision to drug Paulie was wrong. Months later, when the divorce calmed down, everyone's heads cleared.

Paulie was taken off the drugs and he is now doing very well. What he needed in his time of stress was some psychological counseling. He shouldn't have been subjected to the vitriolic behavior of both parents. As soon as the parents calmed down, so did he.

Many times siblings at home suffer torture either

physical or mental by older siblings. In the home environment they are powerless to defend themselves. At school they can feel grownup by dishing out this inappropriate behavior to younger less powerful students. They can have a small moment of power in a powerless life.

If a child is bullying on the school yard, the educator must question the child as to where he is picking up this behavior. If it's coming from home, If he is a victim, there are counseling programs that the whole family can participate in.

A child that is being mentally or physically tortured at home does not need behavior masking drugs, he needs the torture to STOP.

- 6 -
EYESIGHT AND ADD

According to *Natural Health Magazine,* 73% of the children labeled as having a learning disability, such as dyslexia or ADD, have a vision-related problem.

Dr. Hillier, the official optometrist for the USA Olympic Team located in Del Mar California, states, "The vision care myth is that 20/20 is perfect vision. That's not correct, but that's what's checked at school." He goes on to say, "It's completely inappropriate to diagnose ADD or dyslexia before ruling out with tests to make sure the problem is not vision related."

Problems with eyesight can cause a child to be restless, not wanting to sit and do schoolwork for long periods of time. The problem can be as simple as a pair of glasses with the wrong prescription or a stigmatism, to a more subtle problem such as sight processing.

When a child has a problem with sight processing he may test 20/20 but cannot get the messages to the brain properly. The child will seem to be barely able to read. He may hold his head at an odd angle when trying to read.

Children with this sight processing problem are often labeled learning disabled and/or ADD. The ADD diagnosis comes from the frustration of trying so hard and being taunted by classmates. It causes the child to fidget, misbehave and even explode. The child knows he's trying, but no one will believe him. The frustration a child can feel when wrongly accused of not trying can be devastating when the child knows he is trying.

One of the cures is stress relieving lenses. The glasses optically move the print farther away. This allows the eye muscles to relax and move more fluidly.

Wearing stress relieving glasses can jump the reading level a grade or more. It's not uncommon for a reading level to jump two grade levels with the proper vision therapy. The child can also do exercises that teach him how to focus and absorb information. Some children need to school their eye muscles.

For information on how to arrange a vision function screening test call PAVE (Parents Active for Vision Education) toll-free at 1-800-728-3988.

- 7 -
PHYSICIAN HEAL THYSELF

Before attempting to cure a child thought to be ADD (ADHD or ADLD) the parent must truly assess the adult dietary patterns of the household. Does the parent like sugary treats? Caffeine based soda pop? Is the refrigerator full of soda pop leaving no room for the all important milk?

Although some eating habits seem to be inherited, usually they are environmentally passed from parent to child. If the parent states at the dinner table that he does not like broccoli, then most likely a child or two will pick this up and also not like broccoli like Daddy or Mommy. Conversely, if a parent likes to have candy bars, and keeps them around, the child is also likely to develop a taste for them, wanting to eat what Daddy or Mommy is eating. Children who love their parents want to be just like them.

If the parent knows he also has a problem with sugar, he must not pass this on to the child. The parent must do his dysfunctional eating out of the child's sight, at work or in the car. Don't pass it down the pipe, creating another generation of sugar or soda pop addict.

We can't be perfect, but we can hide our dysfunctional behavior. If you are trying to detox a child, don't keep your sugar in the house. Remove it to work or elsewhere. Play fair with the child. If you say no to him, say no to yourself. If the parent is addicted to soda pop, again have it away from the house, out of the child's sight. The rule is don't bring it in if you don't want it going down the tree to your child.

A parent who smokes marijuana in front of his child will never be able to stop his child from doing so. A parent who smokes cigarettes in front of his children will most likely end up with children who smoke. A parent who sucks down the sugar and soda pop in front of his family will raise children who also suck down sugar and soda pop. This is the child's perception of acceptable adult behavior.

In adolescence, children will try to act as adult as they know how, and any forbidden activity they see their parents doing is always the first one to be adopted by the adolescent to show they are cool.

The biggest problem detoxing a child from sugar addiction is usually the parents denial of their own addiction. Parental acknowledgement is the first step to going to Ground Zero.

- 8 -
WHAT DO I TELL JOHNNY?

When going through a detoxing procedure it's imperative that you let your child know what you are doing. Tell him that you are fixing his diet so his "car" will run better. You are going to find all the foods that are "good gas" for his machine. You're going to get rid of all the bad gas that makes his car "break down".

When your child has his next hyperactivity incident tell him, "Wow, you must have some bad gas in your system right now, your car's really broken down, maybe you should go take a nap and sleep it off."

Children are smart, they are creative, they can imagine themselves as machines. They will grasp the concept of bad gas in their tank. Let them participate with you. Help them become aware of their sensitivity.

At no time tell your child he is being bad. Tell him he's reacting to bad gas. Don't ever let your child think HE is bad. Build up his self esteem. Tell him how glad you are that he's smart, he can help by telling you when he feels cranky, so you can better identify what foods and snacks are bad gas.

If your child goes to a birthday party tell him: "Go to the party and have fun, you can eat the cake. Remember though, the cake is bad gas, when you come home you may be cranky or cry."

When your child comes home from the party, and the sugar low kicks in, point it out to him. Tell him, "Oh dear, that bad gas is making you cranky, let's take a nap and sleep it off."

Put your child to bed. He may cry for awhile, but he will also be thinking about bad gas. Next time he feels a low coming on he may come to you and tell you he's had bad gas and is really cranky.

To go to Ground Zero the whole house has to be cleaned out, and the friends, neighbors and grandparents have to be enlisted to co-operate. Alert the neighborhood media, don't try to do the deprogramming in secret, you'll derail.

- 9 -
CHOOSING CHILD CARE

In this day and age of the obligatory dual working household, as well as the many single parent families, child care is generally a must. Before a parent of a sensitive child decides to put his child into a child care situation there are some important issues which have to be considered.

The main one is: do you want another individual to raise your child? You must realize that no matter how much "quality time" you give your child in the morning and at night, the individual who cares for you child during the day will have an indelible impact on that child's habits and morals. That individual will be taking the majority of responsibility for your child's mental development as well as toilet training etc. A parent can set the policy, but it is the caregiver who must choose to follow through.

Is the caregiver concerned about health and fitness? Is the caregiver understanding of your special child's needs. How many other sensitive children do they have on their roster. Are these children merely taking suppressant drugs, or are any being treated nutritionally? What type of food will they offer your child? Will they give your child sweets during the day surreptitiously, even if you have instructed them not to? Will they smoke around your child? Will your child be breathing secondary smoke all day long?

The thing a parent MUST accept about secondary care givers is that no matter what you ask them to do regarding the care of you child, they are most likely to care for your child the way THEY think best.

The other thing to carefully consider is—who is your child bonding with? A lot of professional parents, households of two high powered working parents, are proud of the fact that they can afford live-in help. It allows them to work in the day and go to all the social functions at night. They must accept the fact that although they are the biological parents, it is more likely that the child will bond with the live in, as that person will be the one who is around to kiss the boo boos and tell the bedtime stories.

Don't be surprised or angry when your child goes to this person instead of you for comfort if he has a choice. Also be very careful that the person you choose to provide fulltime care for your child is someone you respect, and someone you would not mind your child growing up like, because HE WILL.

In the old days the mother or grandmother spent time each day working with the children, helping them learn numbers and letters and reading them stories. Now the good child care centers fill these needs without usurping the affection away from the parents. Because it is their sole occupation, the child care centers can focus on the child's development much better than a mother who also has to run a household and work for a living. How many of us come home from a full day's work with the energy to not only fix dinner, but also teach the children well? We're lucky to have the energy to cook a meal, do laundry and clean up the kitchen before falling into bed.

Nowadays a parent has a choice of Montessori, Kindercare and many other types of child care care centers. If the income is low, the county will assist in child care. One of the best after school programs for school age children is the YMCA. They pick the children up directly from school and take them to a safe nurturing environment. The YMCA not only offers the kids a varied activity schedule, but homework assistance as well. The YMCA also has a good preschool child care program.

The important thing in choosing a child care center is not only cleanliness, but do the children look happy and well nourished? Can you walk in unannounced at any time? Are all the areas clearly accessible? What types of food do they encourage the parents to send to school?

A nursery school that allows junk food and sugary treats in the kid's lunches or gives them anything other than milk or an unsugared fruit juice as a snack drink should be avoided. This type of care center will show up on the children's faces. They will have bad skin color, a tendency to overweight, bad teeth and dark circles under their eyes. Due to bad diet, the children will also have a tendency to misbehave at the center, increasing the chance that the caregivers will be cranky with them.

Make sure the children at the child care center are happy, bright and alert, gregarious and in good physical condition. Any fear of adults denotes less than optimum care.

Another consideration is the ratio of caregivers to children, are the kids raising kids? If there are more than seven children per caregiver, there is a possibility that your child well not be consistently guided and nurtured, and he may tend to just absorb the habits, good or bad, of the other children he spends his day with. If this is the case, the parent better make sure the children his child is spending the day with behave appropriately.

Another important consideration is whether the caregivers communicate with the children easily. Will your child be treated firmly but with respect? Some child care situations are merely individuals who want to justify staying home, and have no interest in actually enhancing the development of their clients. They are merely in it for the money.

When choosing a child care situation you must also decide whether you wish to have your child in a progressive learning situation, or a more play oriented environment. You have the car and the driver's license, you also have the checkbook. The kind of personal care your child will have is entirely in your hands.

- 10 -
CLOTHING COLOR AND YOUR CHILD

An elementary school teacher reports an interesting story. She was patrolling the schoolyard. A class was waiting in line to go in to school. the entire class was waiting quietly except for two boys. The boys, who were not ordinarily rowdy, were kicking and punching each other as well as the other children, and they just wouldn't settle down. After repeatedly telling the boys to stop it, and having no response, the teacher noticed that both boys were wearing bright red sweatshirts.

When the students entered the classroom, the teacher asked the boys to remove their sweatshirts. The boys calmed right down.

According to psychiatrists, the color red can incite violence, and the brain reacts to red very often with hyperactivity, or as one psychologist stated, "Subconsciously the brain tries to escape red and retreat into a more calm color environment."

If your child's behavior at school is hyperactive, think about color. Your child may be more passive dressed in green or blue, hyper if dressed in red, yellow or orange.

The school teacher stated that she could always tell who was likely to act up based on their clothing color. Apparently the color reflects up into the eye of the child, and in those sensitive to color, can cause either adverse or positive reactions depending on what color the child is wearing.

After experimenting with children we have found that,

indeed, children dressed in red, yellow or orange tend to be much more active than those dressed in "cool colors". The safest color for the hyperactive child is tan or gray. These colors are not active colors, nor are they too cold. They are neutral.

Also stay away from active, bold stripes or plaids. These patterns also tend to vibrate the eye and in cases of sensetives cause aggravation and hyperactivity.

- 11 -
HOW TO GIVE YOUR CHILD STRENGTH

Children suffering with ADD (ADHD) syndrome are often outcasts at their schools. Because of their inappropriate behavior, they have great difficulty making friends. The other children stay away from them because the sensitive child is constantly in trouble with the teachers and the other kids don't want to be caught in the crossfire. Because of this, the child will often come home depressed about having no friends, or being cruelly teased by the other children.

It's important for the parent to reinforce with the child that children who are cruel and tease are themselves misbehaving. Tell your child that children who bully generally pick many targets. Talk to him about other kids who are also teased, and why they are singled out.

Unfortunately a side effect of sugar sensitivity is uncontrollable temper. This is the root cause of many schoolyard fights. Sometimes this problem is only solved by taking the child to Ground Zero and stabilizing his system so his highs are lower and his lows are higher.

Make your child aware of his behavior in a positive way: "Oh you had some really bad gas. Do you want to go outside and collect your thoughts?" This approach can help greatly in defusing incidents. Your child will learn to step out of himself and observe his behavior. This will make him a very powerful, productive person in the adult arena.

- 12 -

THE ADD ADOLESCENT, MANAGING THE RAGE

This can be a frightening period of time for a parent. Even a child with no sensitivity to ADD triggers will go off the handle when an adolescent. It's not uncommon for very well adjusted children to feel at times worthless, powerless. The child flails about, lost in an unidentified rage one minute, loving and affectionate the next.

In sixth grade children seem to go through a brain drain. They forget everything they have been taught. They vacillate between wanting independence and taking their stuffed toys to bed. They do homework and forget to turn it in. They forget assignments and test the convenient lie escape. The only difference between a sixth grader and a kindergartner is the size of their shoes.

As the child progresses to seventh and eighth grade the insecurity gets worse. They feel impelled to taunt and deride those different from themselves. The tear down others unmercifully in order to elevate their own self esteem. Anything can trigger the derision from clothing color to behavior to a physical handicap or hair color difference. One day they are the perpetrator, the next the recipient.

Even children who are not sensitive to ADD triggers will fidget, cough and belch in class and at home for effect. This is a natural rite of passage, not behavior requiring chemical intervention.

What is required at this time is extreme parental patience. Magically one day all the misbehavior will cease. Your child will revert to the respectful well behaved child he was in fifth grade.

In order to nurture your child, you must draw a very large circle of love around him. Give him space to collect his thoughts. Put your hands deep in your pockets when your child dishes out extremely rude verbal abuse. Parents have to learn to take very deep breaths, and not return the anger that appears to be directed at them.

Adolescent anger is merely an unfortunate, predictable side effect of the puberty process, similar to the terrible twos. It is indicative of the child striking out to find his own individuality, trying to find his self worth. The parent needs to take a step backward and give the child the freedom to step away and cool off, rather than engaging in all out verbal war with the child. Remember that violence returned merely escalates.

Just like the terrible twos, the parent is best advised not to return the level of anger. This is a crucial learning period for the child. Parental behavior under these circumstances becomes the acceptable adult behavior for the mature child. Do not reinforce the verbal abuse with verbal abuse. Calm the child by rational response, even if you have to break dishes in the garage later in private to release the parental tension.

Child-parent verbal wars account for many homeless children living on the streets of large cities. The momentary rage is so powerful that the parent can mistakenly feed off it, and deliver rage and ultimatums impossible to uphold with a confused transitioning adolescent child.

For a child already sensitive to ADD trigger chemicals, puberty is an extreme gauntlet to cross. Not only do they have the same feelings of a normal developing adolescent, but they are intensely heightened. What might be simple rage in a normal child becomes hopeless suicidal tendencies in sensitives. The parent must stay in tune with the child. If he expresses suicidal tendencies, IMMEDIATELY get the child psychological help as well as testing for all the ADD trigger sensitivities. You child's life might hang in the balance.

The best cure is to forgive and to hug. A forgiven child can bounce back. A hug, when the child will accept it, reinforces the closeness that they still need. They won't have to search for the love and reassurance they really want from the parent through gangs, drugs, alcohol or promiscuous sexual behavior.

- 13 -

SURVIVING THE DOG AND PONY SHOW

Parenting a special child, whether he is ADD or in a wheelchair, can be a very draining life. The parent has to be on guard at all times when the child is young to defuse and protect the child from the ignorant hurtful comments of others. In public people usually do one of two things: they stare at the child, or pretend that he doesn't exist.

Put yourself in the child's place. Say you go into a room and no one will look at you or talk to you. Even worse you catch people looking at you, but the minute they see you looking at them they look away. The alternative is the person who stares at you without acknowledging you as a human being.

Only when you've been on the receiving end do you realize that special people are human beings! They like to talk to people. When they get on an elevator they appreciate a smile from the person who moves to let them on. They really want human contact. They want someone to look into their eyes and acknowledge their humanity.

In consideration of this, a parent of a severely dysfunctional child with ADD will at times be invisible to the rest of the world. As the child stands there in a screaming tantrum in the supermarket others will walk by as if you aren't there. The exception is the inevitable person who thinks you are beating the child, gives you their unwanted comments.

You cannot change the world. You can keep the balance by making sure the next time you get in an elevator with a special person that you look him in the eye and smile, and comment on what a nice or rainy day it is. Give yourself, it will help make up for all the times you and your special child will be invisible.

CASE STUDY
The Special Child

Ricky had a visible disability. He had a birthmark that caused him to look like he had a punk rock hair do. When he was an infant, many times, other parents would assume his mother had cut his hair that way. They would make rude angry comments to the mom.

In a toy store, a Marine sergeant accosted the mother in the check out line and asked her how she could do that (the hair do) to her son. In another public place, a man walked right past them telling his son, in their hearing, that her child had AIDS and to stay away from him. Finally, after being accosted time after time, the mother finally came on the right reply. The next time she was accosted and derided for cutting her son's hair like that, she replied, "I didn't do it, God gave him that hair cut." This reply completely took the wind out of the man's sails, and was a much better way to reply than with the rude answer she felt like giving.

With the child with ADD it's more subtle and more difficult to convince the passerby that the misbehavior is caused by a bad chemical reaction than bad parenting. This is what you will hear often. "If that child was mine, I'd straighten him right out."

Tell the truth. As you hold your sensitive child screaming and flailing, turn to the onlooker and say, "Wow, he's having a very bad reaction to a medication, I'd better get him home." Then in fact get your child out of there and give him some milk or anything else with calcium (nature's sedative) to bring him down.

The parent of a special child will come to appreciate the people who come right up and say, "Wow, what happened to him?" at least with these people you can tell them the real story, and they usually are courageous caring people or they wouldn't have asked in the first place.

The most important thing is not to indicate to your child in any way that he has to hide any aspect of himself. This only conveys to him that he's substandard, which he's not, he's special. All his life he will be special, he needs to learn to cope with it early so he can lead a productive life.

The sensitive ADD child needs to make all of his friends, teachers and associates aware of his situation, so they all can help him avoid the train wrecks. Just as you don't offer a drink to a recovered alcoholic, his peers will know not to offer a sensitive soda pop or candy bar.

The dog-and-pony-show will be a part of his life, he needs to accept and understand it. With the proper diet, in many cases the symptoms will completely disappear.

- 14 -
TRAINING YOUR CHILD TO MISBEHAVE

"I have to buy my kid the candy, otherwise he creates a scene." Congratulations to the parents that have made this statement. They have found out how easy it is to train a child. There have been cases where a child is diagnosed with ADD (ADHD), when it is merely a situation of the child training the parent rather than the parent training the child.

First, if this is the case with your child, don't beat yourself up. You are GOOD parents. You just didn't have the data you need to make informed decisions regarding your child.

Here is the key to parenting:

IF YOU LET YOUR CHILD DO SOMETHING THREE TIMES IT BECOMES A HABIT.

The very FIRST time your your infant reaches for a sweet in the check out line, take a deep breath, gently and firmly pull his hand away saying "No". This is the single most important lesson you will ever teach in your child's life-time. You are teaching him that <u>No is No PERIOD</u>.

You also have to be prepared to look like an ogre to the little old ladies in the checkout line who will implore you to let the poor child have the sweetie.

At first, your child is going to make some noise. You are going to be embarrassed. People are going to look at you accusingly. You must be willing to be the ogre. Remember, it will only take about three times of absolute NOs to train your child that when you say no, you mean no.

The biggest parental fear is of saying no. Whether the parent realizes it or not, when you deny your child, there is a subliminal fear of losing the child's love. THIS WILL NOT HAPPEN. The benefit well outweighs the momentary trauma of the training period. It's your choice: three or four screamers, or not being able to take your child anywhere for eighteen years without having him make you and he look like idiots.

When a child goes on a sudden growth spurt, when they grow out of their clothes overnight, their brain has grown at the same rate. These are the times when all of a sudden your child will start a new behavior, something he has not thought of doing before. At first you may not realize that the trouble your child has landed himself in is new—roubles such as climbing out of the play pen. You'll know that all of a sudden you're chasing your child around the house, and you're scared and mad as hell. This is a typical age that the mom who has been taking her child to work has to confront a good child care provider.

Another milestone is the child not wanting to stay in the high chair or booster seat at the restaurant. At this time the parent needs to reinforce NO by GENTLY holding the child in the seat and verbalizing the command. You will have to persist until the child gives up and sits still. This could take a while, and could involve some angry screaming.

As you are wishing you could disappear under the table from embarrassment, keep reminding yourself, "If I stick to it this time I won't have to do this more than two more times."

If the parent gives in to a screaming child the parent is training the child to scream if it wants something. This can give a false reading of ADD. You're also teaching the child that if he's bored and wants to leave a restaurant and play with Mommy or Daddy in the parking lot, all he has to do is scream. Bright kid.

Remember, when a child is little, you are bigger. If you hold a child GENTLY but FIRMLY in the seat he will eventually give in, he has no choice. When the child decides he is not going to win, he will accept it, calm down and go to another thought. Kids are smart, they know when they're licked. The parent is now on the way to having a child that always gets compliments from strangers for his good behavior.

When a child is screaming, it's hard to think clearly. There is a chemical reaction to an endangered child in the parent. The body has a rush of adrenalin. The muscles prepare for escape, blood leaves the brain and rushes to the escape muscles. The parent will want to stop the trauma at all cost. Sometimes the physical adrenalin reaction is parental flight with the child. Unfortunately, sometimes the parental physical reaction is to strike the child in the misplaced belief that that is a cure for the tantrum. Physical violence, though sometimes causing a momentary lull, trains the child to be physically violent. He will copy his parent's instant knee jerk reactions perceiving them as appropriate adult behavior.

In advance the parent must plan to wade through the screaming, and above all be consistent with the NO. Even if, half way through, you decide "Why Not?", you must NOT give in. The next time the child makes the same request, BEFORE you say yes or no, carefully consider, is this a time to say yes or no? Stop and think when your child makes a request. You don't want to quickly give your child the wrong answer, because what ever is the first answer, must also be the LAST answer.

If you haven't made up your mind about a certain request, tell your child you have to think about it. When you do give your answer, stick to it! "That's a possibility." is a good stall if you haven't decided yet. Too often parents will use "no" as an interim answer until they decide, and then turn right around and say "I guess so". The parent may think this kind of behavior somehow makes them a good guy, but this action trains the child that if he keeps badgering the parent, then there's a good chance of reversing any decision made.

Consistency is the key to a well behaved child. A parent needs to be able to walk into the ice cream store and ask for a napkin to clean their child's face and leave peacefully without buying ice cream. If your child knows that no is the last word, he will accept it, not pull an embarrassing screamer. Before going into the store the parent must communicate to the child that it is ONLY for a napkin, and stick to it.

There is nothing more joyous than having a waiter tell you how well behaved your child is. A restaurant is where the monster will come out in a poorly-trained child. The waiters of the world see so many ill-trained children, that a well behaved toddler is a real event. As your child matures, he will appreciate the compliments, they will reinforce his behavior even more.

In a restaurant the most important thing to work on is "we will leave when we're ALL done." Don't train your child to control your visit. The first time your child reaches the developmental level of "desire to leave" you can expect some fireworks. If at this time you instill the fact that leaving will be done when YOU say so, you will set yourself up to enjoy meals rather than having to remove a noisy undisciplined child from a premises.

This training will also be of great benefit when you have to go somewhere for an extended period with your child. There's no promise the child won't get restless, children have a lot of energy, but at least he won't be an ogre to be around.

If you like to have leisurely meals take a small container of your child's favorite action figures, or for older children a favorite book—something he can play with to occupy him as you finish your meal. Keep this toy kit or book hand in the car.

Keep an eye on your child's mental transitions. When the intellect takes a lunge forward, usually in conjunction with a growth spurt, your child will suddenly try new things. Be prepared for these occasions, and especially at these times of mental advancement, BE CONSISTENT! The mental jumps forward by a developing child usually will catch the parent by surprise. The child who for months has been very well behaved, will all of a sudden be driving you crazy. It takes a minute to realize that the behavior that is making you nuts is new, your child has never experienced in these ways before.

You must ask yourself, is this type of misbehavior new? If it is, it means that your child has reached a new mental plateau, and is ready to try a whole different set of activities suited to his new mental level. The hardest period of all related to this is puberty. The forces a parent has to deal with at this time are compounded by the fact that the child is now, in most cases, as big as an adult, and much less intimidated by the parent. Your only hope for cooperation in this period is a solid base of consistent discipline ingrained into your teenager. If you have been consistent with your child in his youth, he is much more likely to obey you in this chaotic period. If you've let the child run you, you are in for some very rough years.

Remember, children are much more secure with rules and boundaries. Give them consistency, along with allowing them to make their own decisions, and they will be much more likely to make the right ones when they are away from the nest, and your protection is unavailable.

- 15 -
ENFORCING NO

As early as possible, a child must understand the word "NO". When he is a tiny infant, if you do not wish him to do something, gently stop him and say "no". If you are consistent with your training you will amaze other mothers looking on in wonder when your child accepts no in the check out line where the cruel store always chooses to put the candy bars. How many times have you seen a mother give in to a screaming child after two or three No, Nos?

The mother of the screaming child has set herself up for failure, and created her own nightmare. The nightmare began because at some point she found it was easier, less embarrassing, to give in to her child than to stick to her NO. It's not easy to stand firm in the face of an embarrassing screaming tearful child reaching out pitifully for a candy bar or toy. There's always some senior citizen in the line murmuring, "Oh, just let the poor thing have it, dearie!"

At some point the loving parent will have to be prepared to look like a jerk, and drag a crying child out of a store. But isn't one or two of those incidents worth having a child who will accept no the first time, and happily go on to his next thoughts, over a child that creates a scene every time he wants something, and won't take no for an answer?

Here's the drill. Even before your child can talk, he is able to reach out and cry for something. At this point you must gently pull his hand back, and say "no". Then you MUST ignore any further crying or reaching. This is very important. You are training your child that you mean what you say. You are training your child to respect the rules. The parent that says three "nos" and then lets the child have the item in question just to shut him up, is training the child that if he cries long enough he will win. The parent is creating their own nightmare!

When pulling the child's hand away, it is NOT necessary to slap the little hand. Repeated GENTLE hand restraint until the child quits the action, or you are loading him in the car is what is required. Have a stiff upper lip. Every parent has to suffer one or two embarrassing screaming incidents in order to train the well behaved child. Just close your ears to the hundred decibels, and picture a child who minds on the first no, that's what you're building!

YOU MUST WIN, DO NOT GIVE IN! If you are consistent, your child, who is quite bright ,will quickly learn that what you say is what is. It will be a waste of energy for him to cry, and he won't. By the same token, if you tell your child he can do something, no matter how inconvenient it is, you must follow through. He is learning how to behave from you. If you don't keep your word, why should he?

Your child will know that if you say he can do something, he can. He will also know that if you say no, it is no, PERIOD, END OF STORY. You will never have to carry him screaming from a store once he knows the rules. That doesn't mean your child won't ask for things, he will. But he will accept what you say, and you will be proud of him and yourself in the face of all the other children you will see misbehaving in the checkout line.

If you say maybe to your child, your child will know he can continue to persuade, but once you say no, the issue will be over. Because of this, your child will be a joy to be with.

- 16 -
ADD AND YOUR CHILD'S COORDINATION

ADD or a growth spurt?

Some of the most frightening incidents a child remembers are over "spilt milk". When this happens in a public place, the parent is humiliated and gets angry at the child. You hear epitaphs such as "How could you be so stupid!" or "You clumsy oaf!" These phrases indelibly imprint themselves on the child, helping him formulate his opinion of himself. These opinions he will carry with him the rest of his life.

The hyperactive child is much more likely to spill his milk, but a parent needs to come to grips with EXACTLY what is going on when a child spills.

KIDS DON'T ALWAYS KNOW WHERE THEIR HANDS ARE.

Granted, sometimes a spilled glass is due to the child fooling around. No matter why it happens, even before a parent blows up at the child, the child IS HUMILIATED. Though outwardly he may show uncaring behavior, inside he feels inadequate, clumsy. Therefore, it's not necessary for the parent to verbally abuse the child's self esteem, he will do that all by himself. What the child needs is a road up out of the humiliation.

The primary reason a child will spill milk, or break something, or trip, or run into a door is that they ARE GROWING they DON'T KNOW WHERE THEIR HANDS, ARMS, LEGS AND FEET ARE. The faster they grow, the clumsier they become. A thirteen-year-old boy destined to be six foot five will crash through the house like a bulldozer. He is so unaware of the length of his arms and legs, the size of his feet, that he will literally knock pieces of furniture out of his way as he passes by. This is NOT ADD (ADHD) behavior, this is a GROWTH SPURT.

For a child to survive this humiliating period in their life a parent must swallow the epitaphs. Instead get into this habit:

When your child knocks over his milk, or worse, say CALMLY, "Boy your are really growing, your hands aren't where you think they are, are they?"

This will help your child heal his humiliation, and give you space to acknowledge your child's accident without making him wrong. If you can't understand the premise, take a trip down memory lane to a time when you spilled your milk. Remember how bad you felt? With your child you have the opportunity to heal the hurt rather than cast it in stone.

- 17 -
TOILET TRAINING AN ADD CHILD

Toilet training an ADD child is a special challenge. Many times the child is too busy to be distracted with the onerous job of informing the parent and taking the time out to do his business in the bathroom.

The best method is to let the child drive the car and train himself. Let him set the pace.

FIRST RULE: **DO not use 'Stay Dri" training pants or pull ups.**

Let's analyze what makes a child want to toilet train himself. You notice I say train himself? That's because he is the only one who can choose NOT to poop in his pants. The motivating reason for a child to cease the need for a diaper is very simple: discomfort. No training pant can motivate a child. They are not uncomfortable.

What motivates a child not to soil his pants is the knowledge that if he does, he gets to sit around in not only a soggy CLOTH training pant, but his clothes will be soggy as well. Children are smart, much smarter that most of us give them credit for. If they know that taking a pee in their pants is going to make them soggy and gross, then they will make a concerted effort not to do it.

Since the advent of the disposable training pants, the nursery schools are finding themselves having to diaper kids until they are four and five. Many schools surveyed said that the change is directly attributable to the training pants that do not discomfort the child. What possible motivation is there? It's much easier to just wet your pants than it is to have to go to the bathroom. At toddler age few children can easily manipulate their own clothing. It's a big hassle to go to the bathroom. However, when the alternative is to have to stand around on wet soggy clothing, guess what? The motivation is there!

The parent must consider this: there is a specific time when a child is physically and psychologically ready to toilet train himself. Each child is different. Some are early, some are late. There is no rule, and no right or wrong age.

The easiest way to find that time, unique to each individual child, is each morning hold up a diaper in one hand and a CLOTH training pant in the other hand. Say to your child, "Do we want a diaper or big (girl/boy) pants today? The child will initially choose the training pants wanting to be a big (girl/boy). Put them on saying, "When you wear these you have to use the potty, so tell me if you have to go to the bathroom. If you don't, you will get wet and yucky."

Be prepared the first time with a change of clothing and a diaper, plus some clean up materials. Soon your child will have to go to the bathroom. An accident WILL occur. Don't be too speedy noticing the child has wet himself. Give him a chance to truly "experience" the discomfort. When your child makes you aware that he is soiled (and probably crying about it) be sympathetic. Say, "Oh, you forgot to tell me to take you to the bathroom. Look at how wet and yucky your clothes are!" CHEERFULLY clean your child up, and put him in diapers again for the rest of the day.

The next day give your child the choice again. Your child is smart, remember, you child knows that if he is wearing the big boy pants, and if he wets, it will be gross. Each time your child chooses the CLOTH training pants, be prepared for an accident. You will find, however, that the child will go back to the diaper for awhile, and then he will start choosing the "big boys" and cease having accidents.

It is not uncommon for children forced to train too early to have problems with fear of lack of control. Many times this fear leads to stuttering if forced to toilet train before they are physically or psychologically ready.

Isn't it easier to wait until the child is ready, and continue to diaper him, than to try to force him into a behavior that makes twenty times the work for you? A forced behavior that can keep you in a state of misdirected anger at you child. What's easier, to change a diaper, or to have to completely wash and redress your child?

When your child is ready to train, accomplish it quickly by allowing him to wear training gear that allows him to feel soggy, yucky. If you do this it will be over quickly, and on to the next!

- 18 -
ADD AND SURGERY

The ADD child can be explosive in a situation of stress and there is no more stressful situation than a child's surgery. Not only is the child apprehensive, but the parent is frightened as well. This fear the child, especially a sensitive one, picks up and reacts to.

How you prepare you child for his upcoming surgery will affect your relationship with your child for the rest of your life.

It's difficult to prepare a small child for getting a shot, much less a surgery. Most of us are tempted to put off the bad news until the last possible moment. We say things like: "Don't worry, nothing's going to happen," or "It won't hurt." A parent once told his child he was going out for ice cream, and took him to the hospital for surgery instead. That child's trusting relationship with his parent suffered serious credibility damage.

Of Course SOMETHING will happen, and it WILL hurt. When your child comes out of surgery, he will be less likely to trust you if you don't level with him going in. You have to be strong.

As soon as possible tell your child he will be getting a shot. Your child will ask, "Will it hurt?" Say: "It will be a prick, it will feel like this—" At this point LIGHTLY pinch you child's arm. Tell him, "That's how much it will hurt." Tell your child that he must sit VERY still for the shot to work, if he doesn't sit still, the doctor will have to try again.

Kids are smart, they don't want to be hurt. If they fully understand your instructions, they will follow them. With a toddler, do the pinch demonstration at least three or four different times over the space of a few days, so he will be well conditioned when he goes in for his blood work. (This works great for immunizations too!). Even have your child do it to you, to make sure he's got the idea.

At the same time, let your child know it's OK to cry BEFORE, and AFTER the shot, but not during. Explain to him that if he's crying he'll jiggle his arm, and he must hold VERY, VERY still while he's getting the shot, or it WILL hurt. You must let it be OK for your child to cry, he will need the outlet for his unease. Make a game of stopping in the middle of a cry. Have your child pretend to cry, and then stop and take a very deep breath for a minute, then resume crying. This game will allow him to easily tolerate the shot procedure, and kids love to play it.

The loving parent who does not provide his child with the right data going into the laboratory or operating theater will unwittingly injure his child on two levels.

1. Having no forewarning, the child will panic when he sees the needle. It will also be be harder to get blood and much more painful for the child. He will also have to be physically restrained, which is very frightening for a child.

2. The child will be reluctant to believe anything the parent says thereafter, if the parent has tricked him into getting hurt. The next time he is in the same situation, he will be twice as upset.

Most parents mislead their children out of love, not wanting their children to suffer undo anguish. Remember a mentally prepared child will suffer momentary discomfort as opposed to the ongoing distress of believing his parents have purposely lied to him.

The next thing to discuss with your child is the surgery procedure. Tell your child that he will be put to sleep with a sweet dream mask. Imitate the mask with your hand lightly covering your child's nose and mouth. Help your child plan the sweet dream he wants to have in surgery. Let the anesthetist know what your child wants to dream about so he can help your child remind himself as he goes under. The dream should be about a favorite pet, or maybe a visit to Grammy, or even a visit to a toy store.

Tell your child that after he gets out he'll have a new zipper or two, and it may hurt a little bit, but he will get all the jello or ice cream he wants while he's in the hospital. Always give the bad news first, and then follow it up with the pay off. Leave your child with the positive thought, something he can really look forward to.

Dress your child in loose clothing that does not need to be pulled over his head. After surgery he needs the minimum amount of bumping when being dressed.

When your child gets out of surgery, it's not uncommon for him to vomit. If he does, be reassuring, let him know that it's OK, it's expected, and CALMLY (No matter how you feel inside) hold the bucket for him. Be aware in advance that this might happen, and be sure to cover whatever he sits or reclines on until it's safe. And remember, vomiting is not your child's fault, it is a common occurrence. It's also smart to throw a bucket in the car, just in case. Those little bitty basins the hospital supplies are hard to hit in a moving car.

The first time your child is operated on, you will be terrified. You will be afraid to bump him for fear his stitches will fall open. You will be exhausted from lack of sleep worrying about his surgery. You'll probably be hungry, because your stomach is too stressed to eat. I suggest keeping a can of Ensure™ in your bag for you and your spouse. It'll replace some of the vitamins you're burning with stress.

After surgery, each time your child cries your heart

will contract. If the doctor says to bathe you child's wound, don't be afraid, do it thoroughly. If you don't, your child's sutures might be infected, and the surgery will be for nothing. Make notes of all the doctor's orders, follow them carefully. If you're ever afraid to do something, tell the doctor or nurse, they will be able to guide and reassure you.

If your child can communicate verbally, he will understand the ideas we've provided you with, no matter how young he is. Trust your child, and allow him to know that he can trust you.

- 19 -
ADD AND THE WOMB

There's a fifty-fifty chance your pregnancy is unplanned, since we're not all rocket scientists, and many beautiful families are created by accident. The fact that you are reading this book indicates that you have decided to have the child, and are concerned enough about your new child to educate yourself about parenting. You are embarking on an adventure that will last the rest of your life. Let's do it right!

Throughout this book we discuss diet related to ADD triggers. These rules apply to new moms as well. What foods you ingest will directly affect your child.

PROTEIN

The Cedar Sinai Medical Clinic in Los Angeles suggests that a pregnant woman ingest (eat) 80 grams of protein per day along with the calcium, vegetables and fruit that are so important. If the parent can't afford to buy this much meat, soy protein powder is a good replacement as well as legumes and cottage cheese. The protein powder is good because the expectant mother can mix up a shake in the morning with all of her daily protein requirement.

According to the Cedar Sinai Prenatal Clinic, protein is crucial for brain development, especially in the last three months of pregnancy.

FRUIT

When your gynecologist asks you if you you are eating enough fruit, read between the lines. He's really saying that without the correct amount of fruit you will not move your bowels properly, and the poisons will stack up in your lower intestines and affect the health of your child. This is a contributing factor in children that are prone to skin problems and rashes all the way through high school and into adulthood.

CALCIUM

If you hate milk, drink calcium fortified orange juice. If you do not drink enough calcium, the baby will "borrow" it from you. Like the things most kids borrow from their parents, you will not get it back, and you will find your teeth cracking and falling out, not to mention bone deterioration (arthritis and osteoporosis). Of course a child deprived of calcium will also be prone to bone problems, and the agony you will go through with the orthopedic department of the local children's hospital is a thousand times worse that taking adequate calcium during pregnancy.

CIGARETTES AND ALCOHOL

If you smoke cigarettes when you are pregnant you can expect an underweight child with very likely brain damage, not to mention numerous other health problems. Cigarettes restrict oxygen to the blood stream, and deprivation of oxygen affects all aspects of organ development, of producing a healthy child. Alcohol consumption can cause a malformation of the spine called spinal abifida. This is when the child is born with a portion of the spine exposed, generally causing loss of use of the legs and lower body, or in less major cases lifelong uncontrollable bowel movements.

COCAINE

Mothers who use cocaine can expect their children to

have brain damage, nerve damage and excessive health problems. Many of these babies become wards of the state, as the mothers have no desire, or are incapable of giving the babies the intense amount of care they require. At birth these infants must be detoxed, a heartbreaking procedure. It's hard on the child and the parents.

If you use cocaine socially, go to the local children's hospital and view the different birth defects that occur in the cocaine babies. You should clean out your system before starting a family if you don't want to take a chance of having a child with numerous health problems that will be a psychological and financial drain on you for life.

SUGAR AND CAFFEINE

What you eat goes straight to your child. Abusing sugar when pregnant can cause juvenile diabetes as well as other medical disorders. Caffeine is a stimulant, it can affect the nervous system of a developing fetus.

- 20 -

ADD AND COLIC

AKA The Six Week Crankies

There comes a time in an infant's life, it could be six weeks or later, that for some reason the child has a hard time falling asleep. For the mothers that carry their babies in "snugglies", it may not be noticeable in the daytime. (A "snugglie" is a frontal pack that holds the infant.) A baby in a snugglie is a happy camper. At night, however, when the baby is put down in the crib it may cry for hours.

There is no easy way to get through this period. Likewise a lot of colic at this age is misdiagnosed. Colic is an infant physical disorder. The solution is generally thought to be walking the child. Many a parent has taken years off their life walking a child all night and having to work the next day.

If you believe your child has a problem with colic, check with your pediatrician. If there is no discernible health problem, "You put the baby down and let him cry himself to sleep," states respected Encino, California Pediatrician, Dr. Helen Lederer. She goes on to state, "It's OK to feel like you want to throw your child against the wall as long as you don't do it."

Sleep deprivation is a very serious disease of the parents of a newborn. What Dr. Lederer instructs her new parents gives them the space to express their exhaustion and frustration, and releases them from the guilt of letting their tiny newborn cry himself to sleep. He's merely training himself how to fall asleep.

Another trick that works very well is to turn on a vacuum in an adjacent room. The "white noise" it creates usually puts a baby to sleep quickly. The drive in the car also works, but you're just as likely to wake up the child when you get home, and have to start all over. The best solution is to just allow the child to train himself how to go to sleep.

The most important thing to remember is that this is just a developmental stage. It will end. Honest, it will.

The pitfall many parents fall into at this time is that the child trains them to walk all night. Even infants as little a six weeks old are smart. If they can create a scenario where the parent never puts them down they will do it. The crafty infant will discover that at night if he cries he will be held.

As much as the child needs plenty of physical warmth, the parents need to sleep in order to remain sane. A good alternative is to take the baby to bed, hold him while both infant and parent can fall to sleep.

- 21 -
THE FAMILY BED AND ADD

If God had not intended the infant to sleep with the mother, he would have made other feeding provisions. The ultimate in efficiency is to breast feed and allow the infant to share the parent's bed. It is definitely easier to just roll over in your sleep and allow the baby to nurse, than it is to go to a different room, and on the way perhaps have to prepare a bottle.

Put yourselves in your baby's shoes. Where would you rather wake up, in a cold empty, huge room, All BY YOURSELF, or snuggled up with your mom and dad? If mom and dad feel like getting rowdy, they can go to the den or the guest room. Isn't that a small price to pay for the indelible family bonding?

Studies have shown that in the countries where it is the custom to share the family bed with those children that wish to, the families are much more bonded to each other. When the children feel secure enough they will leave on their own accord opting for their own space.

After the child has left the family bed for a more independent situation, don't be surprised if he needs to return occasionally. There could be insecurities bothering him that aren't apparent.

If your child is showing a need to be close, try to get him to open up about what is bothering him. Sometimes all it takes is a sympathetic ear to relieve the pressure, or at least make it more bearable. At all times assure your child that you love him and you do enjoy being close to him.

Children who are allowed to sleep with the parent also are less likely to be thumbsuckers, as they are allowed to hold onto their parent as long as necessary to reinforce their feelings of security. Thumbsucking, as discussed later, is a symptom of lack of parental physical closeness. Before a child can talk, body language is necessary to reassure him. If he spends his life in strollers and cribs, he will need to find a replacement for mother's warmth, usually the thumb or a pacifier.

The snugglie and the family bed are the most powerful ways to raise a secure non-thumb-idolizing or orally-compulsive child.

- 22 -
DRESSING THE ACTIVE INFANT

There is a serious practice going on among mothers. This directly affects the growth and brain development of the infant. This is the practice of dressing children too warmly, and then covering their stroller in a blanket.

There are several reasons for this habit of dress. First, in third world countries, with less adequate health care, and much more prevalent disease, the blanket can protect the infant from a life threatening infection. Second, many mothers dress their children warmly because it keeps them less active, easier to handle.

On warm days over dressing a child can raise the infant's body temperature as high as 104. Prolonged exposure to this temperature can affect the brain, retarding the child. The child's cheeks become flushed and the child becomes limp and lackadaisical. The sure signs of heat prostration.

No matter what your grandmother or mother suggests, be aware of the climate when you dress your child. Do not overdress, or drape the stroller in a blanket. You may be unwittingly causing your child brain damage or worse, you may cause your infant's death from heat prostration.

23

BABY'S DIET - INFANT ADD PREVENTION

The Parent Sets The Rules

When a child is born he is a blank slate, ready to be written on. The first time the parent puts a cookie in his mouth to chew on, the parent is training the child to abuse sugar. The worst offender is an infant's "teething " biscuit.

A new Mother has a choice of what foods she gives her child. SHE IS IN THE DRIVER'S SEAT. All of her child's eating patterns are directly related to her choices. If the mother knows the family has a propensity toward low (efficient) metabolism or ADD sensitivity (especially excessive craving for sugary foods) , then it her responsibility to control the dietary tastes of the infant as he develops to circumvent the desire for those ADD or obesity triggers.

Instead of using a teething biscuit, give the child a piece of raw carrot to gum (lightly cooked and then refrigerated, even frozen if the teething is very painful). When the child is ready for finger foods, make all those foods count. An infant will chew on anything, the tastes of these items will be the tastes he develops an affinity for. This is the best window to develop a craving for good foods such as vegetables. Unfortunately most uninformed new mothers use this window to develop in the infant a taste for sweets via the sugared teething biscuit. Vegetables are preferable to fruit for teething, as the fruit also will set up the taste for sugar later.

In the baby bottle should be milk,apple juice, orange juice, or water. PERIOD. There should never be bottles of any beverage sweetened with sugar. This merely helps the child develop a taste for sugar, and sends him briskly on the way toward ADD Syndrome. It also is very damaging to his first teeth, and if the first teeth are damaged the second will come in wrong.

Never give a child a baby bottle or pacifier in lieu of physical warmth. Remember infants cry for five things—in order of importance):

A. **Illness or discomfort -** take your child to the doctor if you can't find the trigger. **BABIES DETERIORATE VERY QUICKLY IF ILL.**
B. **Food** - Milk (Milk provides fluid as well.)
C. **Physical Warmth** - When a child needs to be held put him in a snugglie or hold him, otherwise he will find a surroget for his affections, usually a thumb or food.
E. **Sleep** - Put him to bed, or give him a rock until asleep.
F. **A Diaper** - Change it.
G. **The Six Week Crankies**. A developmental stage where it is very difficult for the baby to go to sleep, many times misdiagnosed as colic. White noise is very helpful at this time. (Refer to Chapter on ADD and Colic.)

Infants that are given enough physical warmth by the parent will not need to suck their thumbs or over eat. They will not need to abuse sugar of caffeine to fill the gap of lack of parental warmth. A busy mom can provide warmth easily with the assistance of a snugglie.

When the infant grows too big for a snugglie the parents must still be available for hugs when the child needs them. They usually don't last long and they prevent a child from feeling the need, especially in puberty, of looking for love in all the wrong places. If the child is getting enough love, physical warmth, and hugs at home, they will be much less likely to abuse sugary foods as a substitute. Later as they mature they will have self esteem, and not have to resort to promiscuous or deviant behavior to fill the chasm left by lack of parental warmth.

Remember, it is the parent who trains the child to love the pacifier or bottle for food or oral gratification. When the child wants to be held the parent should hold the child, not just automatically stick a cold impersonal pacifier or a bottle in it's mouth. The child WILL come to perceive the bottle or pacifier as love, which is why it's so difficult to wean some children from the bottle or pacifier. The parent is removing his only love and comfort.

When the child starts being able to eat solid foods, be religious about reading the labels of the baby food containers. There are a an amazing number of them that carry sugar as the first or second ingredient. If the parent feeds these foods, he is training his child to prefer sugary or sugar based foods.

Provide lots of chewable vegetables as finger foods for your child. Put parsley (a great blood scrubber) on his plate. All foods he is allowed to eat in this time will create his likes later. Whatever you put on his plate, he will stick in his mouth.

A WARNING

There are some vegetables that just taste awful if overcooked. The texture is slimy, and the taste becomes bitter. If your child shows a NATURAL dislike (is not just parroting Mommy or Daddy) for a particular vegetable, back off immediately. There are such a variety available the child can be offered suitable nutritional substitutes.

Don't fall into the trap of pushing your taste on the child. Give him a fair chance. As a toddler he has no external input as to what he should like or dislike. Steamed broccoli is an extremely healthy food. Even if you don't like it because of your upbringing, at least give your child a chance to develop dynamic eating habits.

Most people who don't like broccoli were either presented with it as a soggy overcooked mess when they were infants or the broccoli-hater grew up in a house where a parent was verbal about their dislike of broccoli, and adopted the eating pattern.

Broccoli is truly disgusting if overcooked. It should never be cooked so long it looses it's bright green color. No vegetable should be cooked long enough to loose its bright color. With the departure of the color also goes the vitamins and fiber.

It is the parent who trains the child to abuse sugary foods as early as in the first year. This same parent must confront the onerous task of deprogramming the child when they become older and show that they are ADD sensitive, or become overweight.

- 24 -
SETTING YOUR GOALS

Going to Ground Zero with your child will not be an easy task. You will have to log carefully everything your child eats at meals and for snacks. This includes snacks at neighbor's homes. You will have to make neighbors aware of your campaign, so they will not give your child the wrong foods surreptitiously, negating the work you are trying to do.

You will need to become comfortable with the fact that many people will think you're overreacting. Like unreformed drug addicts, they will surreptitiously slip a treat to your child. In their mind they will think you're being mean. Usually this will be perpetrated by the grandparents or the dietary dysfunctional neighbors.

You need to set timeline goals, and stick to them. Schedule exactly when you plan to have all foods out of the house that can trigger ADD.

ADD TRIGGERS ARE FOODS THAT CONTAIN ANY AMOUNT OF SUGAR (IN ANY FORM) OR CAFFEINE.

The deletion of trigger foods is a crucial goal to the success of a Ground Zero journey. Sugar sensitive "actives" will be drawn to those foods as long as they're in the house. The best road to success is to delete them completely.

If you have non-sensitive parents or siblings, they must be brought in on the program in consideration of the sensitive child or adult. It's not fair to expect a sensitive to eat a different diet than the rest of the family. This merely enhances his feeling of difference, separation from the norm. Let everyone participate, they will be healthier for it. If the rest of the family chooses to abuse sugar or caffeine, let them do it away from the house.

Do not deny your child events such as a birthday party with friends. Plan ahead for the sugar high he will be on, and do not plan any activities for the rest of the day. Give him a peaceful time in which to come down from the sugar high.

If you refuse to let your child participate in a party with his friends, or let him go, but refuse to let him eat the sugary treats, it will accentuate his sensitivity, point out to his peers that he is different. This is something that he does not need at this time in his life.

If your child is fussy the next day, give him a calcium fortified drink like milk or orange juice to help him come down from his reaction to the sugar.

- 25 -
GETTING TO GROUND ZERO

In taking a sensitive child to Ground Zero, you must delete all offending food from the child's environment.

THE KITCHEN

Plan time for this. Maybe enlist the help of a sympathetic friend. All packages of food must be surveyed. The following are forms of sugar and trigger ADD type behavior in sensitives:

- Refined sugar
- Raw sugar
- Raw brown sugar
- Light brown sugar (made by adding molasses to sugar)
- Dark brown sugar (made by adding molasses to sugar)
- Molasses
- Maple syrup
- Corn syrup (dark or light)
- Fructose or high fructose (this concentrated sweetener is a stronger trigger than sugar)
- Glucose
- Honey (raw and pasteurized)

The manufacturers are very clever at hiding sugar in their products. Sometimes you will find a cocktail of three different kinds of sugar substance before there is one healthy ingredient. Be aware that the ingredients are listed by volume, the largest is listed first. If the first or second ingredient is a sugar substance or a preservative, this means that the product contains in most cases primarily that substance.

Every food in the kitchen cupboard and refrigerator that contains a type of sugar, or red dye (a proven ADD trigger) must go. Box them up and take it to the local homeless shelter if you can't bring yourself to throw it away.

Once you are used to perusing the sides of boxes, you will find yourself automatically reading the side of every box you buy. Don't trust foods you've been buying for a long time, just because you assume that they are the same they have always been. Cereals have been known to change over the years, adding more sugar and sweeteners to brands that were once unsweetened.

Many households leave hospitality bowls of candy on the coffee table in the living room. These must go. If a parent requires sugary treats, they must keep them in their car and enjoy them to and from, or at work, not in front of the sensitive child. These types of eating habits are passed from parent to child as surely as a child inherits hair color or the shape of his nose.

The hardest goal to achieve is usually teaching the grandparents. They cannot understand why a little treat is bad for Jimmy. They will want to ingratiate themselves to the sensitive child by being the hero that lets him have a little pleasure he's being denied by his mean mom or dad. Grandparents forget that in their day none of the foods regularly around the house were as sugar laden as those today. In those days you added the sugar, it wasn't already in the food.

Grandparents were raised in another era. They showed lovin' with "somethin' from the oven". A sugary treat like pie or cake was an expression of love, not a dangerous addictive drug, as we know it to be today.

A generation ago, the average child had much more exercise. He was more able to burn off the sugar intake. Safety was not a crucial issue, children walked to school instead of being driven. After school children didn't sit for hours in front of video games or surfing computer internets. They rode bikes, played sports and played outdoors every day after school. Nowadays we're much more sedentary while at the same time eating larger amounts of excessively sugared and caffeine-laced foods. The evidence of this is in every school yearbook. They show the severe increase in the amount of overweight children.

THE SUGAR BLUES

As society becomes more and more addicted to sugar and caffeine, it becomes more and more difficult to find packaged foods that do not contain these substances. The cereal aisle should be renamed the dessert aisle, or perhaps the ADD AISLE.

The advertiser forgets to mention that although they are part of the breakfast they have absolutely nothing to do with the nutrition. The nutrition is provided by the glass of milk, glass of orange juice, the banana and the bacon. The sugary cereal is the part that makes the child irrational, constipates him, rots his teeth and causes obesity. That's what part of a "nutritious" breakfast sugared cereals are.

Although bacon provides a minute amount of vitamins and a minimal amount of protein, it is also is a very questionable product. Studies have indicated that the fat and nitrates in bacon are a prime contributor to prostrate cancer, high cholesterol and nitrate poisoning, which causes severe headaches and in sensitives, extreme hyperactivity.

Spaghetti sauce is preserved with sugar, as is ketchup and many salad dressings and sauces. Read the labels.

Snack crackers and soda crackers change to sugar very rapidly in the bloodstream. Considering that carbohydrates turn to sugar in the blood stream, is it any wonder that sugar sensitive individuals have such adverse reactions to high carbohydrate, sugary foods? They are piling sugar on top of sugar.

The extremely sensitive child needs to be weaned off the sugar, and switched over to a menu designed for a diabetic. Fresh vegetables, meat and moderate carbohydrates. No sauce. Serve whole grain bread in place of bleached flour. Bleached flour has only sugar, all the other nutrients are scrubbed out in the bleaching process, that's why white bread doesn't mold. There's nothing in it. You might as well chew on a stick of wood. If you doubt this, think, have you ever seen mold on a bowl of sugar?

All soda pop must leave the house as well as sweetened drinks. Read all labels carefully. If the product contains sugar or caffeine, out it goes. Once you've cleaned out your child's system, and he's behaving normally, you can add these back a little at a time until you see an adverse reaction.

Once you are used to your detoxed child's psychological profile, his reaction to these substances will be more than apparent when they occur.

- 26 -
MAINTENANCE

Once you've brought your household to Ground Zero, it's easy to maintain. You'll start to get a feeling for what foods are on the list, and what are verboten. As your child becomes more and more familiar with his own body and his body's reactions, you'll find he'll freely tell you when he falls off the wagon. If you don't make him feel guilty, and give him the space to mess up every so often, the lines of communication will stay open.

An amusing side effect of Ground Zero programming is that you'll find yourself hearing about the bizarre lunches your child's peers bring to school. The most remarkable I've ever heard was sandwiches made of white bread and chocolate frosting. Amazingly, I've been told of this lunch by more than a few children I've worked with. You'll also hear about the children who come to school with multiple candy bars in their lunch box.

It's so rewarding to see children once termed incorrigibly hyperactive not only functioning normally, but widening their scope and actually paying attention to what is going on in the world around them.

- 27 -

GROUND ZERO DIET NO NOS

The following food list will give the parent an idea of the types of foods they must delete from the household in order to keep a "clean" Ground Zero, non-ADD trigger environment.

BREAKFAST FOODS

Breakfast is the most abused meal in the contemporary diet. Breakfast cereals predominantly contain excessively high amounts of sugar, both in the recipe, and the add ons such as marshmallows and cookie bits. The rule is:

IF IT TASTES LIKE DESSERT, IT IS!

It's no wonder children are arriving at school hypered out, incapable of learning. Their brains are on sugar overload from their "nutritious" breakfast. The following are examples of foods that must be eliminated from the larder. Out of sight, out of mind!

Sweetened cereals
Granolas (sugar or honey sweetened)
Breakfast pastries
Cereal bars (sweetened with sugar or honey)
Pancake syrup (use just butter or margarine)
Sweet rolls
Donuts

LUNCH

Most tomato-based canned products are preserved

with sugar. Unfortunately, these convenience foods are the ones most often fed to young children. The nitrates in lunch meats also can be an ADD trigger to some children. With this era of sedentary living, dessert should be reserved for a treat once a week. Dessert once a day is even too much for sugar sensitive and low (efficient) metabolisms.

NEVER SEND DESERT TO SCHOOL IN THE LUNCH BOX.

Dessert at lunch will hinder the child's scholastic performance. If they need a mid morning or mid afternoon snack in their locker, at least make it cheese and crackers instead of a candy bar! Give the child a fighting chance to excel scholastically.

The following lunch foods contain sugar and can trigger ADD symptoms:

Canned spaghetti
Ravioli
Pizza
Candy bars (common in children's lunches)
Lunchables (with pudding or candy inside)
Salad dressing (watch the contents for sugar)
Peanut butter (read the label!)
Jam sandwiches

DINNER

Surprisingly one of the worst sugar triggers is salad dressing. Look at the bottle. Many times the dressing is preserved like jam, with sugar. Sauces too are prime sugar targets. Look at the sauces on the prepared chicken meals you buy—is there sugar in the recipe?

Move the family to "cleaner" foods, those without sauce. Young children usually do not like ketchup and mustard, let them stay that way, don't encourage them, you're just adding potential ADD triggers to their diets. Here are some dinner foods to stay away from.

Thousand Island dressing
French dressing
Honey mustard dressing (read those labels folks!)
Tomato sauce (read the label before purchasing)
Canned foods (read the label)
Honey roasted ANYTHING
Dessert (go with fresh fruit to avoid ADD triggering)
Soups (read the label)

Once the parent starts reading the labels it will not be surprising that the child has symptoms of ADD. The culminative amount of sugar ingested per day in many families, not even including overt items such as candy bars and dessert, is amazing. It's a miracle the child can even focus long enough to dress himself!

The best defense is to keep a clean Ground Zero pantry. When a child is hungry, he will forage, and he will eat what he finds. If he can only access good clean"Ground Zero foods, that is what he will eat.

Remember, YOU ARE THE PARENT, you have the money, you are the boss. Exercise this privilege!

- 28 -
YOUR CHILDS' METABOLISM

There are two types of metabolism, slow (efficient), and fast (inefficient). The slow metabolism allows the nutrients to stay in the body long enough to absorb every last "BTU" of energy from from every last calorie. The fast metabolism shoots those calories through at such a pace that maybe half the nutrients can be absorbed. At the same time the fast metabolism moves faster, burns much "hotter" taking many more calories to support the system.

As a person ages, the metabolism slows down. Children who grew up in perfect weight will find they need much less food to retain their body size. When a child is an infant, it is much more in tune with it's body's requirements. When the infant's body requires nutrients the infant will cry to be fed. The infant, upon being fed will take as much as it needs and leave the rest, falling asleep.

As a toddler, the parent starts to dictate how much the child needs to ingest. This dictation is not based on what the child indicates it needs, but on what the parent thinks the child needs. This is a big mistake. Who better knows how much it needs to eat than the individual themselves.

Your child will tell you most clearly the speed of it's metabolism by the amount of food it needs to ingest and stay in good body weight. If your child does not desire food, and is not a sick bag of bones, then you should NEVER force feed the child. This child has a slow metabolism. Instead of cramming food down the child, you should celebrate the low food bills you will have.

On the other hand, if the child has an insatiable appetite, you must continue to provide the needed nutrients until the child is satisfied. If the child is not showing a high percentage of fat on their body, then you can be assured your child runs "hot" and will always require more food. The child is telling you that he has a fast, inefficient metabolism and he is not absorbing as much as the food quickly passes through his system. What he is absorbing, he's quickly burning, using up.

For the child with the fast metabolism it is imperative that the food he eats be quality food, as he will need every ounce of nutrition you can provide to build his young body.

Beware the child that is allowed to eat out of boredom. This child will show a layer of fat, and should be cut back on food intake. Remember a fat child is an obese adult.

The child who does not wish to eat MUST NOT be force fed. If you don't think he's eating enough, take him to your pediatrician and let him check your child. If he says your child is in good health then it means your child has a slow, efficient metabolism.

If a parent force feeds a child with a slow metabolism, he will TRAIN the child to OVEREAT and not listen to his own actual nutritional needs. Obesity will set in very early in life and the child will have to confront the heartbreak of dieting and feeling denied all his life.

If the parent lets the child decide the amount he needs to eat, and always provides the child with good quality food, the child will stay in good weight, even though the parent may not understand how the child survives well on so little.

The key is to always make good nutritious food available to the child so that when they are hungry, they are ingesting foods that will make a difference, good "gas" for their cars.

CASE STUDY

The Jones had four children. Two of the children ate like birds. "We had to keep them at the dinner table hours after the rest of the family was finished, it took them forever to clean their plates." The other two children had no problem, they ate whatever was put in front of them, quickly cleaning their plates.

Years later the two children who were kept at the table long after dinner was over, the children that were "force fed", the ones who "ate like birds" are fighting obesity. Both of them are almost 100 pounds overweight. The two who eagerly ate everything in sight are slim and tall.

A good parent does not force his child to clean his plate. A good parent provides good food, and allows the child to eat what he has appetite for. If the child wants to eat light meals and have snacks the parent should go with it. This is a healthy way to eat. As long as the child is in good weight and health the system is working. Trust your child's instinct, as he is the only one who truly knows when he is hungry or satisfied.

If you have provided food and your child isn't hungry, put it away until he is. Keep foraging foods around such as raw vegetables and fruit. Keep good whole grain muffins (not loaded with sugar) for your child to snack on. Make sure that your child gets the opportunity to eat all the important foods each day such as protein, calcium (milk), vegetables and grains.

If both parents tend to carry extra weight, there is a high percentage chance the child will also have a slow, efficient metabolism. In this case be extra attentive to the child's cut off point. Don't serve the child the same portions you serve yourself. Let the child ask for more if he requires it, don't heap the plate and then make him clean it. Start out with small portions, let the child indicate what is enough.

Remember, your job as a parent is to make sure that EVERYTHING that goes into your child's mouth has good nutritional value, giving him the building blocks he needs to construct a strong body. You only have a small window, from birth until the time your child has his own funds to buy his own food. The first 11 or 12 years will set the tone of your child's health and behavior for his entire adulthood.

- 29 -
THE OTHER REASON A CHILD WON'T EAT

Keep track of your child's body rhythm. When your child seems to be hungry all the time, ("What do you mean you're hungry, we just had dinner!"), the chances are he is getting ready for a large growth surge and the body is stockpiling. At this time it is imperative that the child have enough calcium and other nutrients. So often we see children TRAINED out of a preference for milk by their parents, when their bones haven't finished growing. It's so sad to watch a mother feeding an infant soda pop in a baby bottle, when the only thing that should be entering that child is milk and occasionally fruit juice or water.

If you child doesn't seen to want to eat, don't force him. After the stage where a lot of food is ingested the body will need lots of rest, and less food. If you're worried about your child not eating take him to your pediatrician for a check up. If the doctor says your child is in good health, just let your child control the quantity (not quality) of his intake. Remember, a child will crave food until all his nutritional needs are met. If you feed your child a lot of the wrong fast, or junk foods, the child will crave more food than if you allow him to eat good foods.

Many times parents comment, "I'm a single working parent, I barely have the energy to take the child to a fast food restaurant in the evening." It's OK to take your child to a fast food place, but choose for your child the more powerful foods on the menu. ALWAYS choose milk or orange juice, NOT soda pop.

If your child's tastes in food have been properly instilled, he will prefer the broiled chicken or chef's salad to the hamburger. A mom can even cut up the grilled chicken for a toddler. That with the bun, lettuce and tomato and a carton of milk make a very good meal.

At all times remember, you are much bigger, and the child will do as you say unless you have trained your child to scream for what he wants. If your child has been assisted in developing a taste for greens, he will enjoy the chef's salad which is as good as something you can fix at home, containing chicken, cheese and the all important veggies.

If you child wants the kid's meal for the toy, which is most times the case, buy the toy ala carte. They will sell it alone. This allows the child to have what he wants, and the parent the ability to provide a customized meal.

Children not only love finger foods, but can easily manipulate them. That makes the chicken pieces and chef's salad a treat for them. The chef's salad also is a great training ground for love of salad and veggies. At first order it with no dressing and let the child pick what he wants. He will unconsciously eat the lettuce eventually, even if he steers away from it in the beginning.

NEVER MAKE YOUR CHILD CLEAN HIS PLATE IN ORDER TO GET DESSERT! If fed properly with good food your child will eat as much as he requires. Save the sugary treats for Sunday, or Friday night at the movies or perhaps a once a week trip to an ice cream store. Don't leave sugary treats laying about the house. We unconsciously eat them regularly, having no clue the quantity of our intake. With the generally sedentary lifestyles we live in the 90s there is no use metabolically for sugar every day. We can't burn it off, it just stockpiles.

- 30 -
THE PAVLOV TRUCK

The Pavlov Truck. The nemesis of the ADD child is the neighborhood ice cream man. Parents teach their kids at an early age that when they hear the bell they are to come running in the house begging for money. If the parent says no, an unpleasant scene is sure to follow. One can avoid the whole syndrome by NEVER starting to buy your child items from the ice cream man.

If you never get your child into the habit of Pavloving out when he hears the bell, he will be able to stand right next to the truck and there is no trauma. It's much more fun to take your child on a special outing to an ice cream store. The ice cream is of much higher quality, and pound for pound much cheaper. This makes it an event the child and parent can share, rather than an angry confrontation.

If your child is not in the habit of buying items off the ice cream truck there will be no trauma as it passes through the neighborhood. Make sugary treats an outing, not a conditioned response.

The ADD child will go on a sugar high after eating the ice cream, so don't plan any math tests or or other brain intensive activities after the jaunt.

At all times remember ice cream induces a sugar high, and then a crash. If your child is a sugar sensitive he needs to be given ice cream only in a situation where the subsequent hyperactivity and temper tantrum can do no harm. The parent also has to take responsibility. Acknowledge that they were the purveyor of the drug. When the child misbehaves, remind themselves that it was their willingness to let the child have the treat that has created the misbehavior.

- 31 -
DIET ANTIDOTES

In a family of older children it is very difficult to install new dietary patterns. Our most ingrained tastes are set when we are under five years of age. If the parent has created a craving for sugar in a child, it is exceedingly difficult to back track and get the child on a program of good nitration. the child will invariably look upon it as punishment, as before mommy or daddy always rewarded them with sugar.

The best hope is when the older brothers and sisters are different enough in age that they will be off to school and out of the way. Otherwise if the older child is begging for a candy bar, the toddler will also want a candy bar. In essence, the older sibling will help set the dietary patterns of the child.

Starting from scratch with a new infant is the easiest, but remember, the parent has the money and the parent buys. The parent is the dictator about what foods are brought into the house. Until the child has a job of his own, he needs parental consent for every purchase.

The parent must remind himself the he will not lose his child's love if he doesn't fill the house and his stomach with candy. The child may be mad for a moment, but he will appreciate the parent for the rest of his adult life.

You only spend 18 years raising your child, but you will live with them in friendship (hopefully!) for decades and decades and decades.

- 32 -
SUGAR DETOX PROCEDURES

A child going through a sugar detox confronts two things at once: 1) His body has to detox. He has to battle the craving of the sugar. 2) He goes through a psychological detox. All of a sudden his parent is not giving him the sugary treats he is used to.

It's very important for a parent to have a substitute waiting in the wings. The phrase, "Forget the cookie, give me a hug!" is a good one. Too often these days the parent uses the sugary treat in lieu of physical closeness. Later in life the child will turn to a sugary treat whenever he needs comfort, rather than the support of his spouse or family.

When detoxing, after the house is cleaned out, the parent must plan non-sugar oriented activities, things that the child will enjoy, to take his mind off his deprivation. A trip to the bookstore to the children's book section can become just as appreciated as a candy bar, and much longer lasting. The child can bring home an inexpensive book that mommy or daddy gives him. The gift is a treasured item, and as much an expression of love as the momentary high of a candy bar.

An occasional visit to a toy store can not only be a very bonding experience, but educational as well. Before entering the store give the child a set amount of money. Perhaps it is a good-all-month-reward. Let it be an adventure having the child do his own shopping. Stick to the amount, and let the child know how much he needs to keep in reserve for tax. No matter how crazy his choice, applaud him. His taste will refine. Make it clear to him the money is for a toy or a book, not for candy.

- 33 -
DETOXIFICATION FAST (ADULTS ONLY)

Many adults who have abused sugar suffer from chronic constipation. Sugar slows down in the bowel. Sugar-abusing adults often have a tremendous amount of waste material stored in their lower intestine. Waste products move through slowly, hanging up on the old waste material adhering to the walls of the intestine. Because the walls are caked with old material, nutrients can't penetrate so the person feels exhausted from lack of nutrition.

Undigested pieces of sugar, meat and gristle will lodge in nooks and crannies of the intestine, and start to ferment (sugar) or rot (meat), causing foul smelling flatulence, and precancerous lesions, including prostrate cancer. These pockets of waste also catch virus laden materials trying to exit, making it difficult for the subject to recover from colds and flu.

This impacted waste material will cause colds to last longer, and the bacteria that migrates from the intestine into the mouth of the vagina in women, will cause severe, recurring vaginitis.

In order to cleanse the lower intestine out, a detoxification fast is very important. **Before administering the Detoxification Fast, the subject must be given the green flag by their physician for the fast, the subject must be in good health. The Detoxification Fast is not for children**

unless prescribed by a doctor. This Detoxification Fast can help sugar-abusing children that are overweight and suffer from severe constipation, but should ONLY BE ADMINISTERED TO A CHILD WITH A PHYSICIAN'S SUPERVISION. **This is not the parent's decision, it must be made by a doctor.**

If the subject has the symptoms and meets these criteria, he can look forward to changing the entire context of his or her life with the Detoxification Fast.

BEFORE YOU START

Because the amount of sleep a person needs is partially driven by how much work the stomach has to do at night digesting the food of the day, the subject can expect to be awake many more hours than usual on the Detoxification Fast. Expect it and prepare for it.

Don't lie in bed with your eyes open staring at the ceiling, have books and other activities ready for the additional waking hours. The subject must warn his or her spouse that they may be wandering around late at night, don't worry about it. This is a great time to do things that cannot be done in the chaotic daytime, such as writing that first novel.

The subject will be amazed at the additional energy available when the stomach is not burdened with digestion.

A WARNING

The Detoxification Fast is a two-week fast. Do not be tempted to continue longer. It will stress your internal organs, and could be harmful to your health.

PRE FAST DIET

Before the fast begins the subject must prepare their stomach for the lack of food. This entails a week of gradually "softer" and "softer" foods. At the end of the week the subject should be eating only steamed vegetables.

THE POTASSIUM BROTH

During the Detoxification Fast the body will need potassium. If you don't provide potassium you could severely damage your health.

The potassium broth should be readily available in the refrigerator at home or at work, drink it heated instead of tea or coffee, or cold over ice. During the Detoxification Fast the subject will need at least eight large glasses of Potassium broth per day. That's one glass every hour or so during the day.

Potassium Broth Recipe:

4 lbs. fresh potatoes
2 lbs fresh (NOT canned) beets
2 lbs fresh carrots

Cut the tops off the beets and the carrots. Wash all the ingredients. Do not peel the potatoes. Dice all the vegetables into stew-sized pieces. Put them in a large cooking pot well covered with water. Remember you need the broth so don't skimp on the fluid. DO NOT ADD SALT. Bring the mixture to an easy boil. When the potatoes are soft, turn off the heat. Strain the fluid off the mixture and preserve the potassium broth in a glass bottle in the refrigerator. Freeze the cooked vegetables in baggies to use when coming off the fast.

The subject can drink as much of this broth as he desires. At first it will taste bland, but by the end of the fast it will appear to have great flavor. Make more broth as needed.

OTHER THAN WATER, THIS IS THE ONLY FOOD OR DRINK PERMISSIBLE ON THE TWO

WEEK DETOXIFICATION FAST.

THE ENEMA

If the subject is unable to give himself an enema, he must have assistance EVERY morning. A daily morning enema stretches the intestine and allows the impacted old material to move out of the body. This is an imperative requirement in the Detoxification Fast. If the subject does not do the enema while fasting, then the subject will be "living off" the infected ancient material on the intestinal wall and could become ill.

If daily enemas are not possible, then the subject should NOT do the Detoxification Fast.

Before starting the fast the subject needs to have on hand a good, hanging enema kit with an anal spigot (straight with one hole at the end). Do not use packaged enemas as they do not have enough volume, and the chemicals in them may be harmful to the subject's health during a fast, when he has no food in his system.

The enema every morning should be a 3/4 full bag of body temperature water slightly flavored with chamomile tea. The subject needs to position themselves on hands and knees in the bath tub facing away from the enema kit and administer the enema slowly. Use the stop switch on the hose to cut off the flow when the pressure builds and relax. Let the warm water loosen the blockage. When the pressure has eased, continue the flow until the next blockage. It's important to get the water as far up the intestine as possible as long as the pressure is administered slowly and the subject stops whenever there is a feeling of blockage or pressure. If the blockage or pressure doesn't ease after a minute of relaxation, let that be the limit of the enema for that day. The subject will make more progress the next day.

Never administer more than 3/4 of a bag of fluid. If it

is a doctor supervised Detoxification Fast for a child, rely on the doctor to proscribe the amount of the enema, DO NOT exceed this prescription.

If the enema is administered too hot, or too fast it can be harmful to the subject's health. Like a baby bottle, test the water on the arm BEFORE administering the enema. It should feel body temperature. Keep the hand on the off switch on the cord so that the flow can be stopped the moment the subject feels the pressure. Relax and resume when the pressure eases.

When the water has finished entering the intestine, the subject should stay in position and relax until a bowel movement feels imperative. At this time move to the commode and evacuate the bowel.

The subject will be amazed at the material that will exit. The first day or so the material will look like regular bowel material, but as the Detoxification Fast continues it will become dark, slimy and foul-smelling. This is material that has been in the bowel for a long time, as long as years. During the middle of the two week fast, when the subject has only has ingested the high potassium broth for days, this material will still be detaching from the intestinal walls and exiting.

Every morning the enema will expand the intestine knocking the old material loose. During the second week of the Detoxification Fast, after the subject sees the nature of the material stuck inside his intestine, he'll gladly eat a high fiber diet to "sweep" his intestine regularly from then on.

ENDING THE DETOXIFICATION FAST

On the fifteenth day, add some of the cooked vegetables to the potassium broth, making a vegetable soup. The subject can lightly salt the mixture.

If the subject adds regular foods too quickly it will

shock the system and could cause stomach cramping and painful diarrhea. Gradually add more regular foods until the person is back on a regular regimen.

MAINTENANCE

If the person eats enough fiber, he should not have to do the fast again. This means whole grain bread every day—NO white bread. Eat raw vegetables and salad as often as possible. Meat takes a long time to digest, and tends to clog the intestine. If the person likes to eat meat (especially red), he should double up on the fiber to make sure all the undigested meat is pushed through and does not collect in the intestine.

Once the subject has cleaned out his intestine, and keeps it maintained he will be amazed at the ease of his regular morning bowel movement. A clean bowel track also means shorter colds, and minimal or no vaginitis. (Vaginitis can also be spread by a partner with a dirty intestine.)

Some studies have shown that a clean bowel vastly reduces the chance of many kinds of cancer. Logically it makes sense. If there is material stuck in the bowel for years, it's logical that it would negatively impact the health of the subject. The intestine is the doorway for nutrients to enter the blood stream. If the subject keeps it clean the energy level will soar.

Remember, sugar can lodge in the intestine and ferment materials there causing gas and bloating as well as vaginitis and constipation. Once the intestine has been cleaned, a low-sugar diet also helps the subject stay healthy and full of energy.

- 34 -
GOOD LUCK

In running the gauntlet called life, one has to be able to leap tall barriers in a single bound. In climbing up out of the morass of the Attention Deficit Syndromes, one needs to make one small step at a time. Live today, right now, not for tomorrow.

Every moment with every decision, ask yourself, "Is this the best I can do?" Tell yourself it's just one tiny decision, a building block to an excellent life for you and your children.

Remember the investment you make in you and your family's health now will repay you for decades to come.

For additional support, join the

ADD Survivors Club
PO Box 232111
Encinitas CA 92023-2111